Kathy Golski is a painter, best known for her distinctive landscape and portrait studies. She has exhibited widely in Australia, and her work is represented in a number of public, corporate and private collections in Australia, New York and San Francisco.

She is married to anthropologist Wojciech Dabrowski and has four children and three grandchildren.

Watched by Ancestors is her first book.

KATHY GOLSKI

WATCHED BY ANCESTORS

An Australian Family in Papua New Guinea

SCEPTRE

To Numndi, Pella, Ruminj and the Gamegai tribe of Rulna

A Sceptre Book

Published in Australia and New Zealand in 1998
by Hodder Headline Australia Pty Limited
(A member of the Hodder Headline Group)
10–16 South Street, Rydalmere NSW 2116

Copyright © Kathy Golski, 1998

This book is copyright. Apart from any fair dealing for the purposes of private study, research, criticism or review as permitted under the *Copyright Act 1968*, no part may be stored or reproduced by any process without prior written permission. Enquiries should be made to the publisher.

National Library of Australia Cataloguing-in-Publication data

Golski, Kathy.
 Watched by ancestors.
 ISBN 0 7336 0868 X.
 1. Golski, Kathy. 2. Western Highlands Province (Papua New Guinea) – Social life and customs. I. Title.

995.605

Cover design by Antart
Photographs by Wojciech Dabrowski, Mishka Golski and Plaxy McCulloch
Typeset by Bookhouse Digital, Sydney
Printed in Australia by Griffin Press, Adelaide

This project has been assisted by the Commonwealth Government through the Australia Council, its arts, funding and advisory body.

Contents

Preface	**vii**
A Rough Landing	**1**
Tribes and Tribulations	**71**
Three Refugees	**167**
Another Life	**247**
People and Places	**260**
Maps	**264**
Glossary	**266**

Preface

This is the story of my experiences as the *redskin* woman, living in the remote Western Highlands of Papua New Guinea. In 1981, I travelled with my four children, one of them a newborn, to find my husband in a valley obscured from the world around it by mountains and thick mists. We stayed there for two years, the *redskin* family among the black-skinned Gamegai tribe of Rulna.

Somewhere, lurking in the mists, guarding and monitoring the actions and thoughts of the tribesmen down below, lived the ever-vigilant *tipokai* ancestors, the only ones known to have red skin before the arrival of the white man in the 1930s. These spirits could be helpful and protective, saving someone from being hit by a falling tree, or a hut full of people from being buried alive beneath a sudden mudslide during the wet. But they were also known as disciplinarians, who could send down illness or even death to breakers of tribal law. And so I enlisted the support of Olek, the dead father of my three oldest children, as our own *tipokai*. His mysterious reappearance here soon after we arrived, in the very mountains he had trekked through in the 1960s as a young medical patrol officer, seemed to be part of a greater plan. He returned to be with us, and to be the special honorary ancestor, hovering around the *redskin* children when they were in danger.

It wasn't until we had been in Rulna for awhile that I found out what they were calling me and what it meant: *ambkundr*, meaning 'woman with red skin'. I was a bit put out, thinking of myself vainly as being olive-skinned rather than red. But that is how we were all labelled, so, reluctant to take the full responsibility for the redness, we decided that was how the highlanders must have seen the early explorers, Australian men of Irish stock, red faced from the sun and from unaccustomed exertion—the original *redskin*s.

These first *redskin*s, the highlanders had mistaken for their ancestors. That was the only way they could explain the sudden and amazing appearance of different-coloured beings, arriving from the clouds and the mists in aeroplanes—as they saw it, large noisy birds, carrying sticks that caused death and radios that emitted strange, human sounds, which spread fear and intense curiosity.

Anyway, red was the Gamegai colour for mystery. We were as mysterious to them as they were to us, and they watched our rituals as we observed theirs.

Our time there was snatched from our normal life as we became part of this unfound world. When we left, our destinies had already shifted. Life in those mountains had changed us. Voytek, my husband, wrote *Line to Heaven*, his thesis for the Australian National

University. It was the story of how the Gamegai, after the first missionisation, absorbed bits and pieces of Christianity into their own cosmology.

For me, the painter, the return to my beloved dry land where the fiery colours evoke the mystery of the red earth could never make me forget the grey-green highland mists, which still drift about in my mind, smelling of smoke and pig grease, or the early mornings when the red dawn illuminated the veiled mountain tops.

As for my children, the life in Rulna has given them another dimension. When we arrived there Nadya was thirteen, Jan was twelve and Mishka was ten. Rafal was three weeks old. Rafal is now a teenager, and has to remember the first two years of his life through our stories, through Nadya's songs, and through photographs of himself, the white baby of Rulna, or, in the Gamegai's talk, the little *redskin*.

Four years ago Nadya released a hit album in Papua New Guinea, containing songs written by Mishka. The music excited me so much that I went back to my New Guinea diaries and decided to publish them.

A Rough Landing

12 April 1981

The trip to Rulna from Mount Hagen was a live enactment of a recurring nightmare which has had me, time and again, falling backwards off cliffs or driving down roads which plunge into empty space. The track was barely able to hold the Toyota four-wheel drive, which bumped along at a snail's pace, as the mountain fell away from one side of the road, disappearing into clouds. I gripped my precious bundle of baby with one hand, my seat with the other, and occasionally glimpsed the faces of the children in the back, their attention transfixed, as was mine, by the descending mists so close to the grinding wheels of the vehicle.

My stomach ached from the effort of keeping myself braced against the bumps and hairpin bends, from the skating and skidding across bits of rickety bridges spanning river gorges. Voytek controlled the vehicle with a driving skill I had not known he possessed. I looked at this urbane companion of my life, his muscular arms controlling the dancing steering wheel, and in between savage bouts of fear something in me was moved and distracted by this display of elemental masculinity. He looked sideways at me, a flash of intimacy, and I knew why I had come.

But as we approached the bottom, entering our long-awaited valley, the distraction was dispelled as a crowd of mountain people appeared from the dense forests, surging up the track to meet our truck. They were charged with energy; we were already exhausted. I tried to shape up and face what was to come. Voytek didn't stop, but they followed at the same pace as the vehicle and, disguising feelings of doubt and trepidation, I tried to smile and wave, to match their enthusiasm. Then we pulled up abruptly in a clearing off to the left of the car track beside a grass hut covered with red flowers.

Voytek turned to me, taking his hand off the gear lever in order to summon the necessary solemnity. He had prepared this moment in his mind, the romantic presentation of our love nest. 'This,' he said, 'is our house.'

I don't know how it was that I had allowed my fantasies to create for me an actual house, albeit simple and made of cane and thatch but somehow breezy and relaxed, with a corridor, and sunlight filtering through bamboo slats into an atmosphere-filled bedroom. My stomach gave a strange sort of a twist. At first I could only sit in the truck and stare in amazement and disbelief. Our home seemed to be the same height as the Toyota.

My gaze must have registered dismay, as I sensed immediate disappointment in those observing me. Then my good manners resurfaced, surrounded as I was by the eager crowd who must have constructed the hut for us. The look on my face had instantly deflated Voytek, who had supervised the building. His eyes were impatient and anxious. Our delicate intimacy had vanished. I wanted to re-create it. I had to do the right thing, to rescue the situation for myself, for him, for everybody. Protectively covering Rafal, I allowed myself to be helped down by outstretched hands and ushered through the low door of the thatched hut. As we accustomed ourselves to the dark interior we saw that there was a tiny living room and two bed-sized rooms leading off it. The ceiling was low; we could only stand upright in the middle where the thatch pitched. The floor was a mat of woven split bamboo. Underneath the fringe of the thatch, at the front, was a tiny verandah bearing a narrow table and a kerosene camp stove. And that was it. Down a short path set at right angles to the hut was a hole-in-the-ground toilet, with a tiny roof, three walls, and the front open so that the user would have to squat, it appeared, in full view of any curious passer-by.

We were being observed intently, the watching eyes catching light as they waited for my reaction. Submerging my shock, I forced an expression of delight and a few appreciative gestures to respond to the obvious hospitality and expectations. Outside the hut, back in the sunlight, the welcome started in full force.

The crowd had swelled. Hair was being touched and teased, wrists were being shaken in our faces, shouts of greeting were confusing the still, tropical air. Not ready yet to be such celebrities—in fact having made no adjustment whatsoever to being the absolute centre of attention—we struggled to get back into the truck, but not before a wrinkled elder had extracted my baby's dummy to try it out himself. I managed to reclaim it only after he had deftly manoeuvred it back into Rafal's mouth. Well, that was that with dummies. I threw it into the bushes. As we started to move down the track, I noticed a little crowd diving into the undergrowth to retrieve this pink plastic artefact of the culture we had left behind.

•

Two of the tribesmen had met us at the airport. There was Pri, whose handsome chest bore a metal badge on a heavy chain, indicating that he was the Village Court Magistrate. And there was Ruminj who, I noticed after stealing occasional glances at him, did have a strangely noble look, perhaps because of his aquiline nose, his graceful posture and his black beret with its imposing badge stating that he was a 'Committee'. His teeth worried me. When he smiled I saw that they were stained a sort of beetroot colour, and one of the very front ones was missing.

Both men had strong, bare torsos, their upper arms braceletted with finely woven straw bands which nestled between the muscles. Their perfectly tapering waists were girded by wide wooden belts over which, in a panel down the essential front, were draped woven string cloths, making the outfit modest and yet daring. The crack at the back was covered by a bustle of cordyline leaves. Their lightly tattooed faces were daubed with red paint, and they had colour-coordinated red flowers stuck in their armlets.

I had climbed into the jeep beside Pri, sitting in the middle next to Voytek, who was driving. I had Rafal wrapped up on my knee. Voytek had not seen him since the day of his birth. But to my astonishment, after the first burst of joy at the sight of his son, he quickly resumed his preoccupation with the new relations he was attempting to graft onto us. He was anxiously explaining to us that Pri and Ruminj were his new brothers, and therefore mine as well, and uncles to the children. This was how our family was now and we should immediately feel at home with them. It seemed to me the intimate reunion I had fantasised about was going to come between him and his new brothers. They now belonged by his side. We were outsiders. Under scrutiny. Here on approval.

I wanted to behave appropriately, but I was struggling with a surge of resentment at these new people for diverting my husband's attention. My mother–defender instincts became a chorus, telling me that this place was dangerous for the children and that Voytek had become strange in insisting we come here.

The children were sitting in the back with Ruminj, who kept shaking his wrist and exclaiming at them delightedly. Their responses were suspicious. They were trying to adjust in their own way. Then there was the four-hour trip down to the valley to cope with, which I did mainly by shutting my eyes when it seemed certain that the vehicle was about to plunge off the edge of the road or crash through one of those bridges. Better not to see.

Behind us was the utility truck driven by Father Josef, the missionary from Rulna. It provided me with reassurance of sorts, that someone sane and normal-looking like him would also drive on such a road. I had realised with a shock that this new husband of mine could be a dangerous extremist, and that perhaps I had made an irresponsible and selfish decision in committing all of our destinies to him just because I had found him attractive. I suddenly noticed myself half-agreeing with those who had counselled me against this new and exciting love.

Father Josef, on the other hand, the gruff and handsome young Polish priest, appeared practical and competent. He had been kind enough to come with his truck to carry all our trunks of equipment, medicine, books, clothes, my paints and paper—all the things I had thought would bolster us against our unknown fates for the next two years. I did not want to let Father Josef out of my sight.

•

Delivered from our brief encounter with our 'home-to-be', we drove on down the track to where the road came to an end. This was the mission, where we would stay until we had adjusted. I immediately tried to ingratiate myself with Father Josef and with the lay brother, Brother Paul, a jovial Dutchman in his sixties. Brother Paul's glasses were constantly fogged by perspiration which, he said, was caused by his failing heart. He had been sent by the Catholic Mission to Rulna because mainstream mission work in the big centres was considered to be too arduous for a man in his condition. Moreover, the altitude here—800 metres above sea level—was perfect for him.

Perhaps they would invite us to stay with them for the full two years if we were helpful enough. Our beds in the mission were comfortable and clean, with heavy rough red blankets and white linen sheets. The mission had solar-powered electricity and a flushing toilet. It had a bathroom with a shower. It was private. Having seen what awaited me a couple of kilometres up the road I was in no hurry to go back there. I rushed to do the dishes every time and issued surreptitious instructions to the children not to be noisy and to be extremely tidy; in other words, to change their characters completely.

Despite my efforts, however, it wasn't long before I detected signs that our welcome was wearing thin. Rafal was far too noisy, the children scavenged all the biscuits, Nadya got the giggles when Brother Paul said grace before meals. The gentlemanly silence of the two monastics had been devastated. Their food ran out. Their hot water supply ran cool. And my blood ran cold, as I braced myself for inevitable exile.

24 April

I am trying to think positive; to dwell on the romantic aspects of life in this jungle; to embrace risk, as I did when I married Voytek one year ago.

I found him irresistible, this taciturn and moody stranger from Poland. He promised adventure, but his heavy body was like a bulwark, a haven. The intriguing combination seduced me out of my widowhood. The children harboured strong reservations about this successful usurper of their mother and told me so at every opportunity. They ganged up on him, and on me. I tried to please everyone and ended up pleasing no-one, and our attempts at discipline met with mutinous solidarity from them, with me being situated most uncomfortably between the children I knew and the man I didn't really know. But the birth of Rafal and the impending trip to New Guinea seemed to provide the impetus needed towards accepting him as the only possible replacement for their beloved Olek.

They started to cling around Voytek's bulk, painfully withstanding his dismal moods and relaxing when his blue eyes became twinkly. After all, they were extremely grateful to him for providing them with the unheard of opportunity to quit boring school for two years and embark on life in the unknown.

Voytek has been here awhile and is quite used to the place now. He speaks the local pidgin, the inter-tribal trading language which everyone, except the old people, speaks, and he strides out every day to have his discussions with the new relatives, leaving us to go for little walks and instructing us to try not to wreak havoc in the mission.

1 May

The move to the hut did happen because now we are here. I don't think I slept the first couple of nights because it was so dark. The silence was only broken by urgent calls for three-hourly feeds and once by noisy scufflings outside the hut which made me break out in a cold sweat.

I woke Voytek and he sat up in bed feeling around for anything that could double as a weapon. With my face cream in his hand he bravely turned towards the night. In a waking instant he had become my protector. And then we heard a snort, followed by a squeal. Voytek lay down again. 'It's pigs!' he announced. My rapidly beating heart quietened as we snuggled up together, warm and awakened for each other.

I remained awake. My body had been stirred and my soul aroused, moved by the energy of some strange ecstasy. The thought of the known—my beloved family, now so safely asleep in the deep night—combined with the thrill of the unknown and the future which awaited us. We were changing our destinies, coming here, so far from everything familiar to us except each other.

Rulna, 2 May
Dear Mum and Dad

News from another world. You wouldn't believe this place existed unless you came here. I may have passed through such scenes on a film screen, but that's about it. We are living here at the base of this huge mountain, washing in the river, eating strange food, mixing intensively and all the time with stone-age looking people who are just as curious about us as we are about them. No, they're more curious. They take note of every single thing we do. We are a novelty. I never realised before how relaxing it is to be an anonymous nobody.

We live in a grass hut and wake with the first noises of the dawn: yodels from a mountain top, the snorts of foraging pigs, bird calls. We come outside and already there is a little group waiting to have a good look, just as we try to scurry unobserved down the rather easily distinguished path to the loo. 'Good morning,' I say politely. '*Gut mornin tru!*' they chorus in response.

The children are followed everywhere they go by gaggles of boys and girls who shriek with delight at their every move. Their correspondence studies, which I did all that running around to acquire, have remained in their boxes and are now used as stools. I don't have any energy to try to interest them in schoolwork. That's about last on my list at the moment; last after the nappies, trying to find and cook food three times a day on an exploding kerosene stove, wash the tin dishes and mugs, fetch water, boil it to give Rafal, breastfeed him every two hours, keep him cool and mosquito-free. And all this with a constant audience taking in everything I do.

Nadya, Jan and Mishka wander around exploring their new jungle playground, discovering its secret paths, the freshwater springs, the trees carrying ripe paw-paws. They are visiting the houses of their new friends, trying fire-cooked sweet potato and breadfruit segments, learning to appreciate bush snacks—learning the ropes. That must count for some sort of education, don't you think?

You will be happy to know we are going to mass. On Sunday we all went down to the little grass church on the flat floor of the valley. The bell sounded as tribespeople, dressed in their best, appeared in groups, coming from their distant dwellings, emerging from the surrounding forests and converging on the green grassed area around the church. In the church the women and children sit on log seats on one side of the aisle and the men sit on the other.

We break tradition and sit together on the men's side. Father Josef solemnly enters the church, dressed in a white t-shirt, blue shorts with a huge mud stain on the backside, and sandals. He puts on his vestments over the shorts and begins to say the mass in pidgin. His pleasant baritone voice, delivering the sermon, is then translated shrilly into the local talk by a wrinkled middle-aged fellow called Kaip who has a huge medallion somehow stuck to his forehead saying 'Church Leader'. Kaip's translation seems three times longer than Father Josef's taciturn message and is delivered in a deadpan voice. I suspect he slips in a few other topics related more to local matters knowing none of us will be any the wiser; none of us, that is, including Father Josef. The local language here (not pidgin, which we are all trying to decipher) is as fast as the sound of running water. Do you know that apparently there are 700 separate languages in this small country? Well, back to the church.

The women squat, their children occupying

various comfortable positions on their mothers' bodies. The elongated breasts are always available and uncovered for any thirsty child to take a suck. Nobody appears to listen to anything. At least that's no different from home.

I felt unexpectedly self-conscious when, as the service dragged on and the people sang their droning mountain songs which resemble the sound of a thousand beehives, I had to feed Rafal. He was crying and the congregation, unmoved by the sermon, became vitally interested in his plight. It seemed to me as if the whole church was riveted by my reluctant performance. Some turned round, others looked sideways and hid their giggles in their hands. Perhaps they thought before that white women didn't have breasts. Well, now they definitely know they do. Thanks to me.

Outside the church at last, I had to try and protect Rafal from all those trying to cuddle and poke him, marvelling, no doubt, at his podgy white skin.

Their babies have dusky, satin-smooth skin and they stare at me with an unrelenting gaze, while glued to their mothers' bosoms. Many have little grey furry hats and beads, and painted faces. When they sleep their mothers put them in the large net bags called *bilums*, and they curl up at the bottom like little nuts, rocked and cradled as the mother hangs the bag from her head and swings along the track and up the mountain paths. My way of minding my baby seems cumbersome in comparison. I'm actually wondering if I could cut down on some of my routines, simplify things a bit. But I don't know which things to drop at this stage. Don't worry anyway, I'm looking after him. Perhaps he's even put on a little weight?

The weirdest and most wonderful thing happened to me this morning. I was standing outside the hut, alone for once and enjoying the experience. Suddenly I had this very powerful feeling that Olek was there; above, around, I don't know, but he was there. The sensation remained with me. It was too strong to ignore. And then I realised he was telling me that he had been here, in Rulna, when he was on his medical patrol. I was excited and I told the children. They just felt sad that he hadn't come to them. So I said his reason for coming was so as not to lose contact with them, and to look after them while we were here.

And even now, I still feel he's around, although not so intensely. But it's a good feeling. I'm going to bed now. The boys are lying in their little beds underneath nets, reading by the light of hurricane lamps. Voy is out the back with a few men. I can hear his voice and theirs. Nadya is sitting on the floor with her lamp, furiously writing her diary.

What can she be writing, I wonder, to keep her so still and so quiet? She's usually socialising. I'm tired tonight, but I'm waiting to go to bed until the boys are asleep because I'm afraid that they will doze off and the burning lamps could set fire to the nets and the grass huts. The whole thing would go up in a second. Don't worry, we are very careful about fire. Fire is a friend to us here; it cooks our food and provides little islands of light in the black night. Goodnight and love to you all, kisses for Christina and Trev and the boys. Will ring when we get to town.

Kathy

5 May

The first morning in our hut we emerged shyly as we were under close observation, and we struggled with the kerosene stove to prepare breakfast on our tiny verandah. The stove produces explosive clouds of black smoke, strong kerosene smells and eventually a little heat. We are going to have to get used to living publicly, struggling with our equipment and trying to look serene and in control. I made kerosene-flavoured pancakes and offered them around the staring group. The first man I offered them to loved them. He devoured the lot. I had to start all over again.

We are all forcing prolonged smiles to deal with

the constant audience, and I long for the mission and its private coolness, for Father Josef's detachment, his total non-interest in our lives. We are under observation from the time we wake up until these bush people go to sleep. The night drops like a curtain, early, and all action stops. The bush becomes silent. We are the only ones, it seems, with kerosene lamps. Our house is lit up like a beacon in the black mountain. Alone at last we disappear inside with our lights, saved by the night. This is the time we have to ourselves.

6 May

Anniversary of Olek's death. We sat for awhile, having breakfast, thinking about 'the man who flies, beyond the hills, beyond the skies, beyond the very holy mountains...' That was Mishka's poem which we put on Olek's grave. We could have almost been talking to him. He seems to have a presence here. We looked out at the mountains in front of us.

The River Winimp runs in a deep gully in front of the hut, and behind it rise twin mountains, softly rounded like breasts in the smoky sky. Near us are Numndi's and Kints' houses, but we can't see them. One has to walk through the coffee garden, the pandanus groves and up to the small hill, and there they are—perched high, overlooking the river. They are also little straw cottages, but these ones have no floor—just dust, covered with soft leaves and a fire in the middle of the room around which children and old people squat, cooking bits of sweet potato. They come out when we arrive, stooping at the low door, shaking their wrists, looking and laughing. They take little Rafal's white fist until he withdraws it, offended. Numndi takes him from me.

10 May

We've been here a few weeks and I'm not coping all that well. It's a bit beyond me and I don't really see how I can improve things. Rafal is constantly crying when he never seemed to cry before. He may be too hot, but on the other hand my milk could be drying up. Perhaps I'm a bit too nervous and cranky for making milk. I don't know.

One example of the small difficulties which beset me: our toilet, which is too near the house, is already smelly and attracting flies. Trying to grasp screaming Rafal in my arm and perform the squatting feat requires skills which I may never possess. I approach it as I would a major strategy, tormented by useless thoughts of our two fancy bathrooms back home with their flush toilets, patterned tiles and double showers. And the automatic washing machine! We're such a long way from that here. The nappies are getting out of control because I have to go to the river to wash them and I don't seem to have the time to keep doing it.

I've never been great at housework, but with the total absence of mod cons I'm really quite hopeless. There's not even a broom! I gave up on disposable nappies when I saw the amount of space they took up in our rubbish hole and suddenly imagined them— plastic and paper with shit inside—taking over the earth. So I changed back to nappies. What nappies I have left, that is, half of them seem to have disappeared. The children are no use at washing them; they just start wanting to throw up. And Voytek is too busy with his new brothers to attend to our deteriorating domestic debacle.

I feel completely trapped in this futile situation, with not a soul to help me or understand my predicament, friends to ring up and have a moan to. All anyone wants to do here is stare and eat my dwindling food supply and regale me in a language which they seem to think I understand. No-one has ever worked for wages. They are people of the forest and mountains, growing food for their own needs. Their babies have no nappies, just leaves in the bottom of their *bilums*.

Nobody has or needs nappies, clothes or piles of dishes in a plastic bucket. They just cook their sweet potatoes on their hearth fires and give the peels to the pigs. The biggest difference between us is that they create no rubbish. The pigs eat it all. They don't have tins and boxes of food, or exploding kerosene stoves and lights with temperamental mantles, just little fires. There are no radios they can't tune, mattresses that go mouldy and babies that screech for milk. Their babies are always sucking and clutching a breast and they never cry; in fact, they just stare at us too, coldly, while still sucking.

12 May

The women carry bush knives, the men carry axes and they all know how to use them. Unlike me. I am regarded here like a curiosity similar to a visiting dinosaur. My attempts to chop wood attract no help, only unbridled mirth. I wish I had learnt those skills back home. Besieged here as we are in this strange land, encumbered by a lot of equipment which we can't control but without which we cannot function, I am unable to get the idea across that I could use a bit of help.

13 May

We are a tremendous source of entertainment without having the slightest desire to entertain. The children definitely prefer it to school, though. Unmoved by the stench of deteriorating substances, they have agreed to assist me so that I will cease my constant threats to return home. Jan has taken over some of the cooking. He's a good cook and proud of his recipes, his talent having being stimulated by many months of vying with Voytek for dominance of our kitchen at home. But Jan's cooking prowess takes care of one meal here and there, and kids are hungry all the time.

Mishka's role as helper is to entertain Rafal, who already looks around for him. He goes and shows him off to people, making him 'stand'. He even sits the floppy-headed creature on his shoulders and takes him for 'swims' at the river's edge, copying the local method of bathing babies using a large leaf as a basin. Feeling slightly uncomfortable about the security of these excursions, I neverthless go along with it in order to get half an hour to myself for organising and delegating other essential tasks.

Nadya's job is to cart the water and do the dishes, a communal occupation which suits her flamboyant personality. She likes swinging along the track with the big basin on her head, and has already developed a Rulna style. She takes half the day to complete the task, which she has turned into a major social event.

But still the chores multiply like the bacteria which I imagine infest everything. The intense daytime humidity sends food rotten, nappies foul and our sheets mouldy. I still dream of the mission, with its high ceilings and cool privacy.

26 May

Good news at last! For a few kina a week, Numndi has agreed to 'manage' us.

Numndi has a large nose and shrewd eyes, giving him a pleasantly familiar, Semitic look. I feel I may have seen him somewhere before. He is a type I feel comfortable with. Numndi is deliverance. He organises the children to take the dishes to the river and he gets his wife Pella to do the nappies. And now, for another eight kina, Pella wants to help me with Rafal. It's getting better and better. For Pella, it was love at first sight. The tiny boy immediately felt at home in her arms and in her *bilum*. She gazes at him and her deep giggle soothes his anxieties and mine as well. She calls him 'Rapus'. 'Eh, Rapus,' she says softly, and he does one of his smiles for her.

'How did you get Numndi to do this?' I asked Voy, amazed. Voytek said he explained to Numndi that we couldn't manage here unless somebody helped me, and they all wanted us to stay so he agreed, after consultation with his brothers and Kints, to run us as his own private enterprise—whatever that is going to mean.

Numndi's father, Kints, is the grand old man. He looks benign enough but they say he has killed twenty-two men single-handed, and not even in tribal war; to our way of thinking, cold-blooded murder. However, it seems to me that he's not in a killing mood anymore. He has had four wives, two of whom are still living, and many sons: Ruminj, Numndi, Dokta, Moka, Pugga, Kar, Raima, and adopted boys who have grown-up under his protection.

Pella, Numndi's wife, has a soft, shiny face covered

with grey, tattooed patterns, and large, pigeon toed feet. She wears possum fur as an earring, carries a machete, and has two large-eyed, shy little girls, Sana and Greta. They cling to her leg, half-hidden, looking tremulously at me, thinking no doubt I am a weird lady, white, overdressed and awkward in this environment.

Pella's voice is deep and soothing, and nothing appears to ruffle her. I feel soothed by Pella, even though I still can't talk to her. I guess it's a feeling of common womanhood, a silent understanding of the role we both play in life. Pella's eyes are widely spaced and deep-set in her pleasantly broad face. Her body is strong and reliable, at least one third bigger than the wiry Numndi's. The way she can open a can of food in one second, with a flick of her huge machete makes me admire her. I feel that I've made my first female friend.

1 June
Dearest Mum and Dad, and Family

Things are turning funny, so I'm writing it down as it happens.

It's Sunday. They want us to dress for mass, in their gear. I refuse point blank to go barebreasted with a few bits of string slung between my legs, but I do consent to wearing a headband. Nadya too refuses shyly, but we both watch with smug female amusement as all three of our

watched by ancestors

boys abandon themselves to their costume designers. Feathers on the head, fur too, bark belts around the waist, a possum tail hanging from the neck, kina shells, arm bracelets made of thin straw, and . . . ah, here we hesitate.

The boys are refusing to take off their underpants. They look ridiculous with the sides of their underpants protruding from the luxuriant tail of bum leaves which is tucked under the bark belt at the back. The village men wear their ornaments so deftly and gracefully. On the front they wear a panel of cloth woven from bush string, with bits of possum fur spun into the thread, and slung over the wide belt, which I now know is called the *skin dewi*. The buttocks are uncovered. It is actually, when you get used to it, a modest outfit. They look stunning, the full line of the muscular body being visible and yet not a trace of what the children call 'personals'. When they sit down, with a swift touch of the hand the front cloth is whipped deftly down and under. I have never seen any balls or bum here on any child older than six.

So here are our three heroes: white, proud and dressed to the hilt. Voy is definitely too heavy for the outfit. His wonderful protruding chest and gut bulge hairily from above the tight bark belt. Jan and Mishka, however, the skinny boys, slope whitely inwards above the *skin dewi*. Men will be men, Nadya and I say to each other, feeling secretly sorry for the way they look. Ridiculous they might be, but immodest, never. White men must seem funny. What's wrong with the cheeks of a bum or the thighs? It's only the crack that's rude, and the dick. Our boys, however, think that the whole area must be covered. Nadya and I have to agree with them, protecting them from being disrobed. Even underpants are better than that.

14 June

The river is small, a fast mountain stream full of boulders and channels, and the water is very cold. Nadya, Jan and Mishka 'shoot the rapids' on their backsides, with the local children laughing and egging them on. They do the washing, which dries very quickly on the hot rocks. Then they swim around, delighted to provide such successful entertainment by just doing what they would normally do—fool around in the water. They would not attract any such applause for shooting the rapids back home in the Murrumbidgee River.

And while they swim around, one or two garments go missing from the rocks. Just one or two every time. We are getting accustomed to this, slowly, and to the life here. To the curious local people, coming in, squatting on the floor. Kints, the old man, sometimes lies on Mishka's bed for his noonday sleep, or else he chooses the floor, using the bottom rung of the table as a pillow.

watched by ancestors

This position seems to suit him just as well as the bed. I find his sleeping visits reassuring, and sometimes I sleep too, on our cosy bed, with its little wooden window looking out onto the jungle, cool and mysterious in the steamy tropical afternoon.

Kints has been designated as our father now. He looks older than you, Dad, although he probably isn't, but he's wise and gentle, like a father should be. He's a 'big man', like you (not in the physical sense, of course, but neither are you), even though he has no education. But here, in the Western Highlands, his reknown is similar to yours at home. Here, a bigman is one who builds up the strength and reputation of his own tribe. His career and respect within the tribe are built upon the power of his charisma, his ability to influence, his insight, his wisdom. He is trusted.

It was Kints who forged the first contacts with the missionaries and negotiated the special nature of the involvement. His name is huge in the area. Now his body has become thin and the muscles wasted. His eyes are light with his amazing memories. We are becoming used to the sight of him, to his daily visits, to his function in our lives. He is, they all tell us, still consulted on every major issue.

One of Kints' sons, Dokta, is Voytek's closest confidant. Anthropologists call them 'informants' because they inform about the workings of the culture which would otherwise be a total mystery. Dokta is young, no more than twenty, and slender. Lacking the ostentatious muscles of his brothers, he is inward and eloquent. He has the serious, concentrated stoop of an intellectual. Take away the *arse tanget* (bum leaves) and I can just see him wandering through a campus, books under his arm. With absolutely no education as we understand it, some of these people seem so educated in life matters that it makes me wonder why at home we depend so completely on schooling to make people wiser. Perhaps our box of correspondence papers can remain a stool and our kids can pick up some bush wisdom.

It's okay, I'm just teasing. Of course I will start them on their studies. And I still believe in studies. Kisses to everyone and wait for the next letter from another land.

Kathy

16 June

I am still not used to pigs running everywhere out of control and to the local variety of dogs, which I could better describe as whelps of the most emaciated kind. I have to avert my gaze from these creatures. We have a dog—a smart, well-fed black labrador cross called Winimp. Voytek bought him from a missionary in Mount Hagen, and a cat called Kabuga. (That means 'okay' in local language, because she looks okay; well, magnificent in fact, if one compares her to the local skinny, mangy variety.) The main difference between our animals and theirs is that we feed and care for ours.

21 June

I'm finally beginning to understand pidgin. I'm not as easy with it yet as Voy and the children are, but I'm thrilled with my progress. I can engage more in what's going on around me. At least I can say things, even if I have trouble deciphering an answer. Yesterday, when an old man, Wahg, came to me, I greeted him in fluent pidgin and he told me that he needed to borrow a shirt because his pig had fallen down the toilet pit.

Anxious to oblige, but unsure why or how a shirt would help him, I decided that the possession of such a luxury item would distract him from worrying about the poor old pig stuck in the toilet pit. But Wahg just looked at the shirt and continued to ask me for a shirt.

Ah ha! I thought. He needs two shirts so he can knot them together, drop the knotted shirts down the pit, and the pig can grab on to the end and be pulled out. But how, I reasoned, can a mere pig be induced to grab the dangling shirts? The problem was not solving itself, nor was Wahg interested in the second shirt.

Recognising defeat, I summoned Jan from his position on the rock overlooking the track. He listened to Wahg repeating his request for the sixth time. 'Mum,' he said, exasperated with my slowness, 'he needs a torch! "T" here is pronounced as "S"!' Off went Wahg with the torch, and I don't know how the torch was used, but he did bring it back, his pig trotting along behind him looking happy to be able to snort the fresh air once more.

Our hut is on a main thoroughfare, so we're treated to an endless procession of human traffic, stopping, passing, turning, continuing, carrying loads of bananas on their heads, sweet potatoes in other net bags.

There are different types of bananas here. I try to paint them, to remember them. Some are shot with pink, turning almost scarlet. Some are long and very curved. Others are short and light in colour. Their tastes are as exotic as their appearance. Pigs are strung, squealing, on long bamboo poles. Water is carried in bamboo tubes.

Sometimes the passers-by are decorated beautifully, with headdresses. At other times they wear green ferns in their springy hair, or yellow flowers. Some wear perennial t-shirts, no state of deterioration seeming to render the garment unwearable. This custom is particularly appealing for Mishka who has never cared about changing his clothes. He fits in perfectly.

Women walk with their arms crooked, clutching

children sitting on their necks, pulling huge net bags with their heads. Some come to greet us, putting down their loads to shake their wrists, laughing. Some smile shyly, hanging back. I try to say something; we admire each other's babies. You don't need too much language for that.

16 July

We went to Hagen today. We try to go once a fortnight to buy supplies, have a shower and a rest in the hostel. The trips to Hagen are fun, now that I've conquered my terror of that road. The choice, after all, is staying in Rulna forever with no break, or going up the road. It is hectic in Hagen; we have to pack so much into the few hours we are there: get the mail, telephone home, shop for supplies. The town people don't look happy, or friendly. My purse was stolen when I put it on the seat of the car to change a nappy. All it took was one second of non-vigilance. That is Hagen.

Rulna people come with us, jammed in between us and our stuff. They seem to love going to Hagen, but when they arrive they will not leave our side, until we deliver them to the house of their *wantok*, Raima. *Wantok* (literally, 'one talk') means a member of the same clan. You are always obliged to feed and house all your *wantoks* whenever they might feel like imposing their presence on you.

In Hagen the Gamegai look shy and small as they climb out of the car and go towards their *wantok*'s place. All their normal ebullience disappears in the face of the townsfolk. They must feel like bush men here.

19 July

The way back was actually terrible. One of the men we had taken, Moka, was ill, and I took him to the Hagen hospital. The hospital is a set of humble buildings connected by smelly drains, with casualty departments full of miserable humanity: sick, crying babies and mothers, their faces passive with suffering. Using my knowing white woman technique, I managed to get Moka treated. He had hookworm, they said, and gave me the appropriate medication to give to him.

We have all been warned about the dangers of hookworm, which enters the body through the soles of the feet and, if not diagnosed or treated, can affect the vital organs and lead to fatal illness. I constantly scold the children for not wearing shoes, but the example of Moka may be more effective than a thousand lectures.

The nurse in the hospital neglected to tell me that she had also given the medicine to Moka to take direct. He protested at taking my dose, but I bossily insisted on him swallowing it, and finally he did just that. I did not grasp what had happened until halfway back down to Rulna, when I started to quizz Moka. He was vomiting violently, so we had to stop every hundred metres. He looked green through his black skin. In between bouts he seemed barely alive. We were scared. I thought he was going to die from his double dose. A double tragedy. Everybody had told us that if someone died in your vehicle then you were to blame. And highland revenge is something we have all been warned about. Moka is a really nice man, but I confess I was thinking of our own skins during this time.

It was with great relief that I observed him walking past our door the next morning. And then Ko, his wife, brought me some spring onions as a present. '*Yupela bin rousim bikpela sik bilong Moka*,' she told me, acknowledging my role in double dosing the hookworms. 'You've cured Moka's illness.'

23 July—Voytek's birthday

Voytek had to remind me that it was his birthday this morning. I felt bad, but this is one of two things I still forget about him: his birthday and his name day, the feast of St Wojciech. Because he's Polish he celebrates two occasions, and I respond by forgetting both. Then usually a telegram or two arrives from Poland, from other women in his life, putting me at rather a disadvantage. But today I am rescuing myself by organising two ducks from the mission flock, which Numndi will cook in the traditional way, interred in a ground oven—a *mu-mu*, a feast of feasts. And anyway, no telegram can arrive here in Rulna.

24 July

The laws of supply and demand don't really work at Rulna. Either we get ten hands of bananas and two dozen pawpaws at once, or else nothing for a month. The locals are used to growing produce just for themselves, and seem reluctant to sell any of it. The Hagen market is large and colourful. One can buy a *bilum* there or an avocado, a beautiful pig rope, tree tomatoes or bamboo combs which can tweak fuzzy hair and spin it out into a soft cloud. At Rulna there are no fuzzy clouds of hair, though. Hair is cut short, often with the sharp blade of a machete. Afro has not reached the bush.

At Rulna nothing is really for sale, either, although I paid Ko to make bush hats for all of us, at ten kina apiece. They have two corners on top of the head and possum fur spun into the thread. These hats are an integral part of dress in the place where we live and I want to wear one too, to look more at home. I have abandoned my former way of dressing, trousers and stout boots, and now wear a sarong and a pair of sandals.

7 August

Today we went to Ruminj's house. It was raining softly; the paths were muddy and often just a bog. Ruminj walked deftly, lightly, straight through the bogs. We picked our way round, slipping and clambering across two mountain streams. We were getting thirsty with the effort, but Voytek would not let us drink from the cold, tempting water, telling us that with water one can never be sure. He should know; he was in Nepal and Afghanistan, where even the sweetest-looking water was a death carrier. We drank the water, nevertheless, when he wasn't looking because thirst was clouding our vision—and now I feel guilty because I'm sure we will all come down with hepatitis.

Ruminj's house is high up the mountain, all on its own. When we arrived, I caught my breath, shocked at the silent beauty of the place, looking down the mountain at the gardens and the cloudy valley. Ping, Ruminj's wife, squatted humbly in the darkness of the hut, her sad eyes shining with her secrets. Ping was a second-hand wife. Ruminj had got her cheaply because she was a widow, and he always referred to her, cruelly I think, being in the same position myself, as a *lapoon,* an old woman. They call women here *lapoon finis* as soon as they have had children!

Ping has a grown-up son and now two little ones with Ruminj. Bag, the boy, was named after a rice bag; Kina, the girl, after the currency. Naming here seems to be entirely arbitrary. The name of Pri, the Village Court Magistrate, means 'vomit', I believe. He is an elegant and handsome man, the more so because he has nice white teeth, so the name seems incongruous.

Pri's wife keeps deserting him and going back to her people's tribal lands. She says that as Village Court Magistrate he neglects his home duties and never cuts the wood for the fire. He complains that she won't tend the garden and thinks she is a lady, staying at home with their three children. He says she is rude to his friends and won't cook for them.

This all sounds like a normal marital argument, the fight over who does more of the work than the other, but division of labour is strict here and taken for granted. The men prepare the gardens, the women plant and tend them. The men build the houses and cut the firewood; the women cook. The men go to war. Gardens and houses are made only every few years, and tribal war is infrequent, but gardens are tended and harvested the whole time, so, generally speaking, the women's lot is harder.

Men discuss a lot, play cards while sitting in the dust, plan pig exchanges and go to war. On the whole, during peacetime, a relaxed existence. When Pri's wife leaves him and he attempts to inveigle us into assisting him to retrieve her with the help of our Toyota, I am inclined to leave him to his lamentations. When any woman walks out, there is always a good reason. That's what I believe.

Ping prepared us some tapioca, *mamiok*. We tried

to make appreciative expressions, digesting the white substance which resembled, for want of another comparison, school glue. And then Ruminj gave the boys a spear each, beautifully carved and bound. He has enormous dignity in his own surroundings. I asked him if I could go and stay the night at their place, so I could see the dawn break over the mountain, to be there with the first noises of the morning, to catch a little piece of it for my own soul. He just looked at me and smiled his beetroot coloured, gap-toothed smile.

We clambered back, the path steep and our progress alarmingly fast. Slowing down was impossible. I kept reeling down the slopes grabbing branches to stop my swift descent. Ruminj had Rafal tucked safely under one arm, the other balancing the axe over his shoulder. The contrast between Ruminj's swift, deft grace and our breakneck crashing down the hill made me feel powerless and inadequate.

22 August—Nadya's birthday

First thing in the morning there was a big commotion around our house. We wanted to make a birthday breakfast celebration, but first we had to inquire into what exactly was happening. It seems that a young girl was being sued for the alleged theft of a bra which they all said was Nadya's. An unlovely bra of the pink, old-fashioned type which none of us, including Nadya, had seen before was being brandished by a het-up middle-aged man who was speaking at some length in impassioned tones while groups of women with their eternally sucking babies sat around staring at him.

Nadya, embarrassed, rushed purple-faced back into the hut. Numndi explained the situation to us. Outrageous, such a theft. The girl should pay compensation, he said. I went inside, uninterested in the fate of the shabby undergarment—our breakfast party was ruined. The boys, however, engaged in lively discussion with the prosecutors, and Voy produced his notebook, eager as he was for all clues to the workings of this society. Compensation of eight kina was awarded to Nadya, but as court costs amounted to seven kina, Nadya was presented ceremonially with one kina. Well, it was her fourteenth birthday today, so the one kina seemed to be a fitting present from her new gang.

We had our traditional birthday celebration which, though mundane enough to us, caused a gratifying amount of excitement. The iced cake (a train cake because it was made by the boys) was lit up with fourteen candles. We sang the 'Happy Birthday' chant, and then the 'Stolat', the Polish chant, followed by the blowing out of the candles (passing the last lit one around the group) and finally the cutting and division of the cake. Our ritual seems to be as memorable to the Gamegai as when they delight us with their *mu-mus*—their method of cooking for festive occasions. Their pigs are lowered into an oven which they dig in the ground, lining the hole with banana leaves, heated stones, sweet potato, taro and fern fronds. Everything is steamed together in the closed up hole.

We think their *mu-mu* is more impressive than any birthday party we have ever seen.

23 August

Most houses, like Ruminj's, are like retreats. They are nearly all situated high up—small dwellings, strung along the ridges, hidden in isolated spots above the mist line. People live close to their gardens but not really close to each other. During the day they congregate down here, and we have become one of the focal points. Our house, being near Kints', the tiny courthouse, and not far from Pri's, is strategically placed to view the action.

There are a couple of other dwellings beside the one-kilometre track that winds from our place to the mission—the house of Panna the policeman and, next to him, Gabriel Kei the storekeeper. Panna, apart from his badge which says 'Police', displays no other outward sign of his office. Occasionally Panna will show off his handcuffs, which otherwise remain hidden in his small men's *bilum*.

One day when Panna was demonstrating the cuffs to Nadya and she was playing with them, a visiting, more senior police officer arrived on the scene. Outraged at Nadya's disrespectful treatment of these tools of a dignified office, he proceeded to lock them onto her wrists.

I arrived in time to see Mishka standing and making a formal plea for his sister's release while Nadya sat humbly with her head bowed. I rushed inside to suppress my laughter, just as Mishka was settling the compensation to the officials—four cigarettes each, which Jan proceeded solemnly to hand around. Situation averted. But it occurred to me that I would love to have a pair of handcuffs to use myself, to lead the giggling Nadya back to our house.

2 September

We have just got back from Hagen, where we collected Kate who has come to stay with us for a few weeks. She lived near Hagen as a child, with her father Jack Golson who was doing archaeological research on earlier civilisations. The research revealed that as long as 9000 years ago there was a highly developed community in Hagen with an advanced and centralised water drainage system. Now there are only individually dug drains around the gardens.

Kate, who has just left school, has exciting memories of her childhood in Kuk, the site of the dig where her family lived.

Today, as we arrived back, a man came with a large

leaf on his shoulder, covering a disgusting looking abscess, and called for Dokta Miki. For Mishka has become a sort of mini doctor. He has acquired a box of dressings and other bits and pieces—tweezers, disinfectants, scissors—and with cool aplomb he applies them to wounds that would make me turn away in horror. His reputation has spread through the mountains, and he has developed his own clientele.

Standing on his stool to achieve a workable height, Mishka coolly attended to the man's wound. He gently peeled back the leaf, which seemed to carry a fair portion of the infected shoulder with it, placing in its stead one of our familiar and trusted white cloth dressings. The leaf, the man explained, is a nettle leaf (*nuntz*) whose various curative properties include drawing out the pus. Well, it sure did that.

Burns on children and knife wounds are Dokta Miki's area of expertise. Illnesses he refers to the *haus sik* attached to the mission, a small house with a tin roof and concrete floor which is manned by a trained medical worker. Dokta Mikel Kewa deals effectively with emergencies and illnesses which would seem to be way beyond the orbit of his brief training. He has two assistants, and now he supplies his outpost—Dokta Miki—with materials which are kept in a lock-up box.

It amazes me to see the sudden connection between the young Dokta Miki and his dead father, Olek, a real doctor—the same calm concentration in the face of illness and distress, the same warm humour, banishing panic in its wake. He even looks the same. He advances upon the scene with the same measured gait and inspects the problem with a specific tilt of the head of which I am suddenly reminded, seeing it again.

15 September

The Mabege tribe inhabit the mysterious dark mountains adjoining the lower heel of our valley. They have been traditional enemies of our Gamegai group for several generations and it is said that it is dangerous for Gamegai to walk in Mabege territory. Nonetheless, Jan and Kate went on an exploration of Mabege country with Voytek, and when Kate got back she told Nadya about Gris, the beautiful young son of the bigman. He had been their guide.

Almost upon completion of the story, Gris arrived at our place. Nadya saw him coming across the bridge. He approached confidently on the single log, watching her as she did the washing on the rocks below the bridge. He grinned at her. He was wearing a *skin dewi* and *bal* (front panel of the *skin dewi*) which, she observed, had been folded short, as he'd come to Rulna all the way across the mountains from the Mabege territory. His shortened *bal* revealed his muscular and (Nadya noticed regretfully) 'splayed' legs. His *bal* was very clean and he was wearing a couple of leaves in his hair. As he finished crossing the bridge she saw that his *tanget* (bum) leaves were fresh and bouncy. The muscular legs, the fresh *tanget* and Gris's huge smile made her finish her washing quickly and hurry back home, carrying the dish of wet clothes on her head. There he was, standing over an injured bird with me. The bird's mother had been shot down by a catapult, in the endless search for feathers, and the infant had been brought to the children, who asked Gris to save it. He seemed uninterested in helping the bird and said that he had to go back to his own territory.

Nadya, a nubile fourteen who seems to have assimilated instantly in the short time we have been here, has incorporated the news of her love for Gris into songs which she and her friends sing on the rocks. The songs ring out, chorus and response, and the sound rises and falls away with the wind or with the noise of the river. But the word 'Gris' is repeated over and over like a mantra.

Gris has received news of the songs and has started regular visits to Rulna. Yesterday he brought a present: live eels inside a woven bush trap, and bush turkeys' eggs which, when broken into the pan, yielded bloody fledgling bush turkeys with closed eyes and skinny necks.

'Yuck,' shrieked Nadya, for whom the delicacy was intended. 'I'm not eating blood and guts!' The impasse was solved by Ruminj and Numndi, who were only too pleased to consume the bloody morsels. They both forgave Gris immediately for being a Mabege, reassuring us that the generosity he displayed in presenting such a gift more than offset the fact that he was from an enemy tribe. In fact, they said, he would be a very suitable boyfriend for Nadya.

20 September

We are building a new house—*haus Nadya*, everybody calls it. It is a simple process. The upright poles, roughly hewn, are dug into the ground, and the ceiling beams are nailed into position. *Kunai* grass, the grass which grows as high as sugar cane, is cut and brought up from the bottom of the valley, carried in great sheaves on the women's heads. This is their job, the cutting and the bearing of the *kunai*, the thatch grass for the roof. Long, soft cane grass called *pit pit* is brought down the road from the tops of the mountains where it grows. We bring it in our car. It is beaten out and woven into panels which are nailed into place to form walls. *Haus Nadya* is for Nadya and Kate. The little verandah is the correspondence corner, the schoolroom. The construction of the house takes four days.

21 September

My birthday. Today I am forty. Nobody has remembered, but for me the day has not passed unnoticed.

watched by ancestors

They've all gone bush for the day with Voytek and I'm sitting here alone. It is a situation I would normally welcome. Out would come my paints and my paper, and a peace would descend on me as I gave myself over to the totally involving process of solving the riddles of the light on the leaves and trying to make my paint cooperate with the paper. Painting weaves its magical space around me.

But today I can't paint. I feel sad and forgotten. I have the curious thought that perhaps, with no mail and no phone, I could escape this terrifying mile post altogether. Then tears well up in my throat as I open the floodgates to thoughts of being not only forty, and married to a man in his thirties—that's bad enough—but also completely uncelebrated on this day of days.

I am imagining the fuss that would surround such an event back home: a great party, champagne, presents, flowers, congratulations. The house would be in a pleasant turmoil, preparing to look its best, as the fireplace lived and crackled. The long table, soft with candlelight, would be laden with dishes made by Jan and Voytek in their ongoing competition for the laurels bestowed by me on the best feast-maker. (I always try to declare them equal, and fail miserably as a judge.) Here I will scrounge around for enough rice and sweet potato, the normal rations for the day.

Numndi looks at me, curious. In vain I attempt to enlighten him. His total non-comprehension of my poignant situation is actually making me feel better.

He has no idea how old he is. Nor does he care how old I am, and he really cannot see why I care. I stop crying and start painting.

22 September

The day wore on and they all came back and nobody paid any special attention to me, although they were a bit upset that I was still painting and had not provided a meal for them to fall upon greedily. I started again to feel a bit tearful, and even like breaking the momentous news to them, so that they could all feel suitably ashamed for forgetting a creature so pivotal to them and start rushing into the preparations which would be considered suitable for such a calamitous event.

I opted instead for the sweet temptation of martyrdom. I made their dinner, wordlessly, and ate nothing myself. I lived inside my head, which had become a warm ocean of self-pity. The evening passed, I remained thirty-nine, and slept frostily away from Voytek, who wondered at my strange mood, as the tears seeped stubbornly from the corners of my closed eyes. He had enjoyed his day and wanted to tell me about it; I had not responded and I was determined not to respond. The touch of his hand on my shoulder made me feel worse, because it felt tender and I longed to be able to curl into his body.

But I was determined upon my course, and I still

am. I have decided that none of them will know until the arrival of the next mailbag, and then the vision of their shame will be my sweet reward for martyrdom. Parents never forget their daughters' birthdays.

23 September

Of course I told them. I couldn't wait until the birthday greetings from the mailbag broke the news. It is just not in my nature to be so patient. So they made me a little post-birthday party, train cake and all. Now I am forty. And I'm relieved to be acting myself again with all of them, and to be able to cuddle Voytek, instead of lying stiff and strange beside him, not even telling him the reason.

30 September

There is a *sing sing* in Tigi and a huge delegation is walking up the mountain to join in the festivities which surround the *moka*, the ritual giving of pigs by one tribe to another. This establishes parity between the tribes and, for the forseeable future, peaceful relations. Tribal war is feared here, and known by all. Numndi's name means 'lone survivor of tribal war', indicating that when he was born they were hemmed in by enemies. This time it will be the Gamegai giving pigs to the Menimbi tribe, who also inhabit Tigi.

Numndi says he will escort the children and Kate. They will go by foot up the mountain path to the top side of the Wahgi-Sepik Range, where Tigi is situated and where the other half of the Gamegai tribe have their lands. Voy and I will drive there with Rafal and whoever can squash themselves into our Toyota. Numndi has prepared a pack of food and jumpers, because it is cold 'on top'. We are all going to wake up at dawn to wave the walkers goodbye, for it will be a long journey. We will leave a few hours later and hope that we find them.

3 October

Now we are back at Rulna, the contrast with the last few days at Tigi making Rulna more sweet, more clean, more luxurious than it really is.

Tigi started off well. We found the children and Kate on top of the mountains, near Numndi's father-in-law's house. They were exhausted, but exhilarated after the long trek. They had white mountain flowers in their hair and were sitting with strangers by the side of the high mountain road, framed by the rising mists from the valley below. It was somehow dreamlike to come across them in this way, with no warning that they would be there, with people we had never met, on a road we had never driven, against a view we had never seen. And with flowers in their hair.

We went to the *sing sing* ground where we were

allotted a hut on the side of the cleared ground. We made the place cosy with our hurricane lamp, spreading blankets on the ground, filling our empty bellies with stodgy tinned meat. And then the skies burst, and it started to rain, and rain, and rain. And there we were, stuck in the hut in the middle of a huge sea of mud. No toilet, no water tank, marooned.

We put our muddy boots on the tiny verandah overnight. In the morning one of Voytek's and one of Mishka's were missing. Voy, furious, attempted with one boot on and the other boot off to summon the local councillor to complain about this shabby treatment of guests. But his complaint had little impact. The councillor made a few sad gestures of deep shock and sympathy and that was that. Voytek paced the hut, bootless, raging. Mishka ran barefoot into the squelching mud.

It was I who found the two mismatched boots, half-filled with rain, planted behind our car. The thief, evidently disappointed with the bad size match, had dumped them. All day long, rain notwithstanding, the pig donors, the main celebrants of this *sing sing*, surged round and round in front of our hut, brandishing spears, painted literally to the eyeballs, and singing. Others, including our children, danced with them in circles, arms over shoulders, singing and chanting, the mud mixing with sweat and rain. When pigs are given to another tribe in *moka* they are not simply handed over, but presented after an amazing season of dancing and commotion.

By night we were all covered in the mud. It had been walked into the hut, it was on our blankets, our clothing, our food. I was acutely homesick for Rulna and resolved never to venture out again. Our food supplies had been demolished and Rafal had settled on a steady wail which he could maintain with minimum effort ensuring maximum irritation from those around.

The night was filled with the droning sounds of the *tanim het* ceremony, the courting ritual which was taking place in the hut nearest ours. The meeting of two tribes always provokes these love ceremonies, which to me are more beautiful than the stamping, shouting, emblazoned warriors, the colourful frenzy of the *moka*.

In the smoky darkness of the hut where the ceremony is, the glowing embers of the fire provide enough light to partly illuminate the faces of the couple, enhancing the surrounding gloom. Young men sitting on their haunches, sway one or two at a time, in circular rhythmic movements, rubbing noses with the secretive looking, heavily beaded virgin seated beside the embers. All around, the onlookers chant the courting songs, their strong voices falling in cadences and then swelling again in a minor key. All night they sit there, the boy changing position, the girl remaining constant until the first light appears.

I had arrived at the ceremony with Voytek when the children were asleep, slipping through the dark mud towards the sound of the droning. We had entered discreetly, trying not to disturb the trance-like atmosphere. Sometime before first light I went back to my hard piece of floor. Voytek stayed.

Today he drove us back down to Rulna. I am completely fed up with Tigi, but he has returned at the insistence of the Gamegai men. Voytek, they told me sternly, has to *tanim het* too, because whereas women when they marry become 'has beens' (that's me, of course), men are still free to pursue other women; at least, they say, until their beards are grey. What horrible traitors they are to me, these men I thought were my friends. I am jealous and hurt, wanting him to stay with me, not go chasing other women, even for research purposes. So I barely wished him goodbye. I just turned my back on him as he left and came inside to write my diary, choking back bitter tears. I wish his beard was grey. I wish I wasn't here. I wish he was, I wish, I wish...

4 October

Now to my work. Since Pella has been helping me with Rafal and Kate has been forcing the children to do their correspondence, and since they spend a lot of the morning washing the dishes and the clothes in the river, I am finding time to set up my little studio. It is quite basic. A *kunai* roof over a *ruminj* (centre pole), a drum on which to rest my paper board, and a stool. Pigs, chooks and children wander in and out.

I'm finding my way in. The solitude of the last twenty-four hours has worked on me. My soul is saturated with my new surroundings, and there is something germinating in me, linking me with this ancient valley which has mysteriously become my home. Its inhabitants are as integral a part of the place as the smoky hollows, the birds and the graceful breadfruit trees which pose, like dancers, all around our hut.

I am weaving my own space and at the same time forging connections between myself and the environment, taking a bit for myself. This is what painting does for me; it links me to a place or to a person. Sometimes the connecting process is jerky and difficult, at others it flows strong and intoxicating.

Voytek has come back, stimulated by his experience, wanting to tell me about it, to boast about his reception with the Tigi virgins in the courting ceremony. I managed to remain surly and uninterested for awhile, but I had to steel myself to hide the fact that I was really relieved and happy to see him again.

Voytek, ready for my coolness, was sweet and flirtatious. I happily went to the river with him to wash, and we sat for a long time in the rapids, our backs pushed against the surging cold water. He 'shampooed' my hair for me with Sunlight soap. It doesn't lather the hair, but I liked him doing it anyway, and my skin feels like silk after sitting in the fast river.

Rulna has its luxuries, and the river is one of them. The other is the sweetness of being together in the river until the mountain casts its great shadow over the singing water.

5 October

Tropical ulcers have taproots. A small cut or scratch, even a mosquito bite, can turn into an ulcer which burrows its way right through the flesh to the bone if it is not checked. Our salt-water soaking routine half works, but first I have to drag the children from their jungle playground to institute this time-consuming and tedious procedure three times a day. I sometimes resort to antibiotics.

Nadya and Kate get the most. Their legs are marked all over with purple pit marks. Jan, in addition, has developed a severe rash, which will not go away despite a variety of local cures, and remedies that I have learned from my new bible, a book called *Where There Is No Doctor*. I have dosed him with antihistamines, and now not only is he rashy, he is also drowsy. I just wish he would return to normal. The antihistamines stop the furious itching but the personality change is unnerving. My normally lively and alert boy has become sleepy and unresponsive. He keeps lying down to doze. There has to be another solution.

Voytek tells me that rashes like Jan's actually killed

many people in Jim Taylor's first expedition to explore the Hagen area. 'It is from sensitivity to a plant, probably *kunai* grass,' remembers Voy, stirring my worst fears of mortality and loss.

Jan scratches and the scratches become ulcers. It looks serious. Voytek's information about the condition gives me the night fears. I continue to stuff Jan with antihistamines, not knowing what else to do. But his uncharacteristic sluggishness is as frightening for me as is the rash. We will have to take him to the hospital in Hagen, to wait with all those desperate people. Illness here strikes suddenly, and seems more mysterious, more acute.

9 October

A couple of days ago I woke and found I couldn't stand up. My body, normally so competent and reliable, had betrayed me. When I did finally manage to rise, I almost immediately wobbled back to bed. I was so ill I thought death must be near. The children panicked, and argued with each other and with Voytek about what to do with me. Voytek had been given some penicillin injections by a doctor friend in Australia and he wanted to try one on me, but he could not quite remember where on the body he had been advised to inject it in order to avoid paralysis. This problem, extensively discussed in my presence, scarcely disturbed me. I just didn't care.

I was detached, and almost uninterested in my fate.

I just wanted Jan to deal with Rafal. I was too sick to feed him but I didn't want to hear his screams. Voytek went to get a *dokta* to take a blood sample for a malaria test, and he returned after some time with Wamp, Mikel Kewa's assistant, from the *haus sik*. Wamp, young, nervous, naked from the waist up, and with a head full of white duck feathers, pierced my finger with a razor to take blood for a smear (smears, I had heard, rarely leave Rulna for analysis). Then I mustered what strength I had left to resist Voytek's injection which Wamp was recommending. Dokta Miki, leafing through my *Where There Is No Doctor* and taking my case history, diagnosed my illness as mastitis and began treatment according to the book's directions. Fortunately we had the appropriate antibiotic in our kit.

For two days I was the centre of a nervous, hovering crowd, all begging me to feel better and to start functioning again. I had stopped being there for them, withdrawing into my own strange world, for once lacking the energy to even care what they were doing. They wanted me to return, healthy and present. Rafal adopted his low-gear, persistent wail. He was hungry, his milk supply had gone, and he was sceptical of Jan's attempts to jolly him up.

But now I have recovered and Rafal's cries have subsided. Jan's rash persists; however, relieved for a few days from being overdosed by me on antihistamines, he has recovered his exuberant personality (even if he does scratch himself until he draws blood).

10 October

We took Kate into Hagen for her flight home, and Jan to the hospital. The doctor gave him cream and cortisone tablets, which cured him. After Kate left we drove back down to Rulna, and that night the rains came, the river breaking its banks with a great roar. It came right along the road, past Kints' house, black, furious and full of banging, crashing boulders. Mishka was afraid. He stayed in the *haus kuk*, our little shelter with its cooking fire, sitting on Numndi's crossed legs and listening to everyone tell flood stories. Raima said that not since he was a small boy had he witnessed such a flood.

This, they told us, was the beginning of the wet season. The big rain, following the burning of a house, they said, signalled the arrival of the wet. I couldn't work out whose house had burnt down, but I was thankful it wasn't ours or Numndi's.

Nadya, ever active and never afraid, rushed to the edge of the torrent and her new yellow gumboots immediately filled up with mud. I spanked her and pushed her into her room, helped by my new friend and ally, Gris. Nadya cannot bear him anymore, ever since he 'dobbed' on her for stealing Voytek's beer and sharing it with her friends in her room. That's what she says, but I'm sure it also has something to do with her fickle heart which has rejected him for having 'splayed' legs, a fact she keeps mentioning. He watches her mournfully, failing to understand why his report on her misdemeanours should have such severe repercussions. He has now become Jan and Mishka's firm friend. They are very upset at what they regard as Nadya's unjust treatment of a good man and they think his legs are just fine. I feel the same, although at the beginning of this romance I had reservations about his acceptability as a first boyfriend. I simply could not get past the fact that he could neither read nor write.

11 October

Moka brought us a bird, a baby bird. Its mother, no doubt, was yet another victim of the eternal quest for bright head feathers. 'It eats grasshoppers,' he told us, helpfully. *Kints*, I have learnt, means 'grasshopper'. I find this information unhelpful, even if I have interpreted him right, as I have never, in all my time here, seen even one grasshopper. And if I were to see any, I could not imagine myself catching one. And my attempts at asking people to find a *kints* inevitably end with someone calling out for Kints, who then arrives, expectant.

So Dokta Miki, being the animal man, has become responsible for the bird. Well, he has been able to track down a few grasshoppers, having wisely solicited the assistance of the boy Agena. Dokta Miki is always clever.

Nadya and the boys watched today as Agena fed

the bird on worms and grasshoppers. Then this evening Nadya asked me if she could be excused from doing the dishes in order to do a little schoolwork. I was immediately suspicious, but nevertheless had to agree with this virtuous request from someone normally so unscholarly. After she went to sleep I just sneaked over there to see what sort of work had been achieved. Beside the table were several pieces of screwed-up paper. On top of the desk remained a couple of sheets of lined foolscap. One bore the formal title 'The Bird':

> *This jungle is written all over your face*
> *And even the way you move*
> *This bird is yours*
> *And its feathers belong to the jungle*
> *Even the way it flies.*

Could this mean love? The night is steamy and unsettled. I went to bed but could not sleep, so I crept quietly out to the verandah and lit the lamp, to write. I am thinking about the poem, but not about the bird. It is my daughter who occupies my thoughts.

13 October—Mishka's birthday

Trust Mishka to be born on the thirteenth. And today, on his eleventh birthday, the rain stubbornly drummed down on our little hut, refusing the sun even a few minutes to dance its shadows around and make the raindrops glisten. But we celebrated. Everyone is prepared now for the candle ceremony and the cake. And the cake had to be a train again.

It seems our birthday parties will always follow this set format from now on, misleading the local population with regard to the permanent presence of the train. We are trapped in our ritual as it has been observed and remembered.

20 October

Voytek has gone to the Jimmi Valley, accompanying Father Josef on one of his periodic visits to that region below the furthest hills. This is Voytek's second visit there. The Jimmi people speak a different language from the Hageners. They have other customs. Sweet temptation for an anthropologist. He will reappear in a few days, paler and thinner but exhilarated. He likes Father Josef and they have good times down there despite the physical hardships. They talk in Polish, exercising the beloved language again. When they come back I will have a feast waiting for Voytek, and clean clothes and some whisky. And Brother Paul will have a feast waiting for Father Josef. They are received like heroes. One day we will go, I tell the children. We will be heroes too.

The Jimmi has grown, in our imaginations, to exotic proportions: a land where the gardens are huge and plentiful, the houses built high on stilts, and coconuts grow; a land beyond the great Jimmi River, spanned by the swing bridge all made of bush rope vines, *rop kunda*. The Jimmi people are small and not as beautiful as these tribes, being subject to virulent malarias and skin diseases. They all die very young and their children have huge, swollen spleens. There are no grandparents down there; they die before achieving this status. The Jimmi is two days walk from here (walking eight hours a day) and is lower, more tropical, not blessed by the cold nights which make us huddle inside blankets here in Rulna.

21 October

The wet season is difficult. People's moods change. Everyone is always sheltering from the rain, from the storms. The joyful washing sessions beside the river are cut short. The river has turned brown and unfriendly. The gloom sets in early in the afternoon and we have to light the lamps.

We are confined to our own huts now, and we have to live together at close quarters. I find myself more snappy and irritable. The clothes are never quite dry. We save them up for our trips to Hagen. But last time we tried to go to Hagen the car kept getting bogged, and was blocked by landslides. Constant earthquakes send whole slices of mountain tumbling over the road. It takes two or three hours now, to dig two tracks for the wheels over the top of the landslide if it is not too severe. Then we tie a rope to the front bumper and all haul on the rope as Voy tries to drive over the top, his wheels in the freshly dug tracks. One slip the wrong way could take the car right down the mountainside. There seems to be no choice but to take the hideous risk. Turning back just never seems to be an option that occurs to us.

The last trip we made to Hagen, just before Voytek left for the Jimmi, was one of these digging marathons. It seemed to be essential to continue because Voy had arranged to meet an official from the Australian Department of Immigration at the Hagen Park Hotel in order to officially receive his Australian citizenship. There was no way of sending a telegram to the man: *Sorry stop blocked by landslides stop unable to attend meeting end*. The sinister powers of Immigration can manifest themselves in cruel ways if the bureaucratic requirements are not met. So we risked lives to continue rather than invite the retributive actions of the institutional giant.

In addition to a landslide, the large supporting beams of the bridges were rotten from the wet, and some of the slats had been stolen, presumably for firewood, making the many water crossings precarious. We crossed on foot, leaving Voytek to manoeuvre the car along, at first driving very slowly and then zooming up towards the other side and skidding to a stop on terra firma. I watched through my fingers till he was over.

We got to the meeting place in Hagen. On time.

'You know what, Kot?'

'What?'

'Maybe I don't want to be bloody Australian after all.'

'Voy!' I was shrieking. 'We've risked our lives to come here! You've got to do it!'

He started to look stubborn. I forced the tone in my voice right down and tried to sound calm and reasonable, because I knew his stubborn look, and I also knew that the more frantic I got the more he would refuse to budge from whatever unreasonable position he'd chosen to adopt.

And then he did it. It took all of ten minutes, and he emerged as an Australian. And we returned, singing 'Waltzing Matilda' as we drove down the track in the rain.

26 October

Our lives inside the hut are taking a different shape. Voytek is still away. We have many visitors during the day, refugees from the rain, people coming for diversion, entertainment. The evenings start early and sometimes plagues of moths darken the air and cover our food, flying around the lights. I have learnt to eat stolidly, pretending the moths are an exotic sauce. The children refuse to eat the moth sauce, Mishka claiming that he wouldn't dream of eating moths 'alive'.

watched by ancestors

28 October

The boys have invented two board games to pass their evenings. Jan, in his confident creative way, has drawn up the boards and made the tokens and dice. He has painted the stories onto the board. Mishka has had a large say in the Book of Rules. They play quietly until there is a huge conflict about 'the rules'. Accusations of cheating fly backwards and forwards, the grass walls of the hut shake as they push and wrestle with each other, Numndi rushes in and separates them, and then the rules are rewritten in a way less open to manipulative interpretation.

One of the games, called Tribal War, has tiny doll tokens made of wood, with faces painted the colours of the different tribes, like club colours. The dolls have shields and wooden belts. Jan spreads out his paints and wood carving tools and sits for hours, his curtain of thick dark hair hiding his face as he stoops over his work, rapt with concentration.

Nadya is only interested in her friends, her giggling girlfriends. She has become one of them. There is Moni, Pella's younger sister, and Meri Meta. She gossips with them, and gives them her jewellery, which is really mine. My furious protests are treated with utter contempt. Her friends, she points out, give their jewellery to her, so it's fair.

'Black rubber wristbands from kerosene tins, Nadya, are hardly a fair swap for a gold chain and a turquoise bracelet which your father gave me! Nadya!'

But she is gone before she can even hear me. She puts her hands over her ears. She runs faster than me. I am left, gasping with fury and the futility of chasing her through the jungle and making an ugly scene as I demand that the receivers of the jewellery return it. Anyway, I was stupid to have brought it here. What did I think I was coming to?

Nadya often sleeps in Numndi's house with the women and children, curled up together on the floor. The men sleep at the other end of the hut. Thank goodness, I think. Because for sure she would be looking out for a casual visit from the boy Agena, the one with 'the jungle written all over his face'.

At Numndi's house they all talk and chatter and wake at first light to stir up the fire and cook the sweet potato, cut into long strips and toasted on the embers. Nadya comes home, pinches our tea and sugar and back she goes with her bounty. Their day has begun before the rosy dawn softens the low-lying mists.

I am continuing to transfer my feelings about my environment onto paper—to work out new ways of painting the changing mists and shapes, the colours and shadows of the leaves of banana, pandanas and breadfruit. The breadfruit leaves, large as coolies' hats and deeply indented, capture a never-ending variety of hues as the changing light transforms them.

I paint the mothers and children who squat on our little verandah waiting for a break in the rain so that they can hitch up their loads and continue home.

They bend against the weather, their large splayed toes gripping the steep muddy surfaces of the mountain tracks. I paint and chat, scrutinising the mysterious calligraphy of the soft facial tattoos, peeping at the babies, self-sufficient and aloof, as they survey me unblinkingly from the comfortable curves of their mothers' bodies.

We live in gumboots now, and have bought a large umbrella with the Shell company logo imprinted on the side. It has to be hidden after its every exposure because it is a desirable item, and such items go missing. Umbrellas are more effective than the traditional way of keeping dry, which is a banana leaf cover, or, more recently, a bit of yellow plastic.

29 October

Rafal is crawling. He is eight months old. No longer content to sit in Pella's lap, he wants to roam, to explore the mud. In vain I try to make barriers on the edges of his sheet of plastic, to make it a sort of playpen. It doesn't work. He insists on his right to join the primeval slush. *Malu malu*, they call mud here, a term of endearment meaning 'soft'. Rafal thinks the same. He wants to play in the mud and enjoy its softness. He wants to slosh it all over his face and hair and would love to eat it too if possible. I won't let him. He screams and stretches his arms towards the forbidden territory. Oh, wet season, when will you end?

But the wet season has only just begun.

1 November

Jan has made friends with Rot, who now comes to visit, suggesting little excursions with Jan to collect feathers or bark for bush belts. The two of them go off together up the mountain, returning in the evening. Rot has been ostracised by his own family group because he made trouble for them by flaunting his affair with Maria, the sultry Rulna widow. Without any handing over of pigs from the man's kin to the woman's kin, no relationship is properly recognised here. Pigs were given for Rot's current wife, but Rot does not care for her. He has eyes only for the saucy Maria.

Maria has also been punished by her deceased husband's kinsfolk, who have taken away her four-year-old child because, they claimed, she was poisoning the child by breastfeeding at the same time as having intercourse with Rot. This is one of the beliefs around here, that having intercourse while breastfeeding threatens the child's life.

Maria's keenly interested brothers surprised her in the act of loving Rot, and did a sort of on-the-spot forensic test on her which they cited as proof that she was both giving herself away without a brideprice, therefore depriving them of their pigs, and at the same time poisoning her child. Anyway, now she is pregnant, and the handsome Rot is obviously the father-to-be.

They look like a very happy couple, despite the setbacks. They even hold hands, which is pretty radical behaviour for Rulna. Maria looks enticing, notwithstanding a missing tooth. She has a heavily tattooed face, a cigarette permanently stuck on her bottom lip, and a very naughty grin.

She nevertheless shatters the romance of it all for me by telling me that her former husband was beautiful and tall, and so much better than Rot in every way. I express surprise at her lack of delicacy, and tell her I think Rot is good-looking. He is. I try to tease her, jokingly, saying that most women would think the same. I have told her before that I was suddenly widowed, and that Voytek is my second husband, and that love can be wonderful the second time around, when one is a little more experienced; it's just different. But she laughs flirtatiously, unconvinced by my advice, and insists that Rot is a 'humbug' (a person not to be taken seriously).

Mishka was listening to one of our conversations. He said he agreed with me, although he told Maria that he used to think Voytek was a 'humbug' too, but as his own father died and won't be coming back he can't imagine anyone other than Voytek doing Olek's job. And anyway, Voytek must be pretty good, bringing him here.

'What sort of woman would you like to marry, Mishka?' I asked.

'One like Pella,' he said. 'I would like to marry Pella.'

'Why Pella?' I asked, surprised. Maria was laughing. 'She's married to Numndi!'

'Numndi doesn't mind if I marry her too. I already asked him. I like her because she's strong.'

4 November

Voytek returned from the Jimmi. I saw him trudging up the path, coming out of the mist and the rain. Quick, where's the whisky? Make some food, Jan. But Voytek was not in a greeting mood. He stumbled in and flopped on the bed, not bothering to take off his wet, steaming clothes. He was ill. Malaria.

'Mishka! Get the chloroquine!'

I peeled off his stinking garments, removed his boots and putrid socks. And as I cradled his feverish head in my lap, bathing it with tepid water, I was thanking God, or rather *tipokai* Olek, for allowing Voytek to get here before collapsing. Dokta Miki administered the chloroquine—four tablets—Nadya fetched some tea, Jan made some food. Slowly the fever subsided. Once again, Rulna, and our little hut, was a haven of safety, a home.

The next day, however, the malaria returned.

Voytek's body was shuddering violently. His teeth were chattering. The chloroquine was not doing its job. I had to get him to Hagen, but there was no way I could negotiate that road, especially in the wet. Nobody in Rulna had a driving licence. Father Josef was just back from the Jimmi, but I had to ask him. There was no other way. A delegation was sent off to the mission with a note.

Father Josef instantly agreed. The two men had become friends during the long march. Voytek could hardly get himself to the vehicle. Father Josef helped. Fortunately, the road was clear and the trip uneventful. I was really praying for that. We left the three older children with Numndi, putting the responsibile Jan in charge, and took only Rafal. The trip seemed to take longer than usual, even though there were no landslides.

I dropped Father Josef in town and went to the hospital, where I burst into the casualty department but was immediately blocked by long lines of waiting patients. One man had a spear in his side and lay gasping with pain as his relatives wailed around him. I ignored them and pushed my way to the doctor, a fellow Australian, pleading with him to come out to the car to see my drastically sick husband.

'Look! I can't just leave these patients to go and attend to your husband in the carpark. Is anyone sicker than these people here?' He gestured around, indicating the sick child he was with. He looked exhausted. I started to crumple. I was exhausted too.

Rafal, on my hip, started to wail. I didn't know what else to do, so I stood my ground.

He explained to me, while treating the child, that it was no use taking a blood sample to test for malaria, because the chloroquine Voytek had been given would be masking the parasites. The best thing, he said, was just to treat it as if it were a resistant strain. He asked a nurse to fetch the appropriate medication plus a glass of water and I took them out to the car and administered them to the shivering heap of Voytek, curled up in the front seat.

We checked into the hostel and he started to recover. But we stayed the night anyway, enjoying the clean sheets, the cooked dinner, warm showers and fluffy white towels. We collected Father Josef, bought a load of chocolate for the children, hoping that they still existed, and hit the road for Rulna.

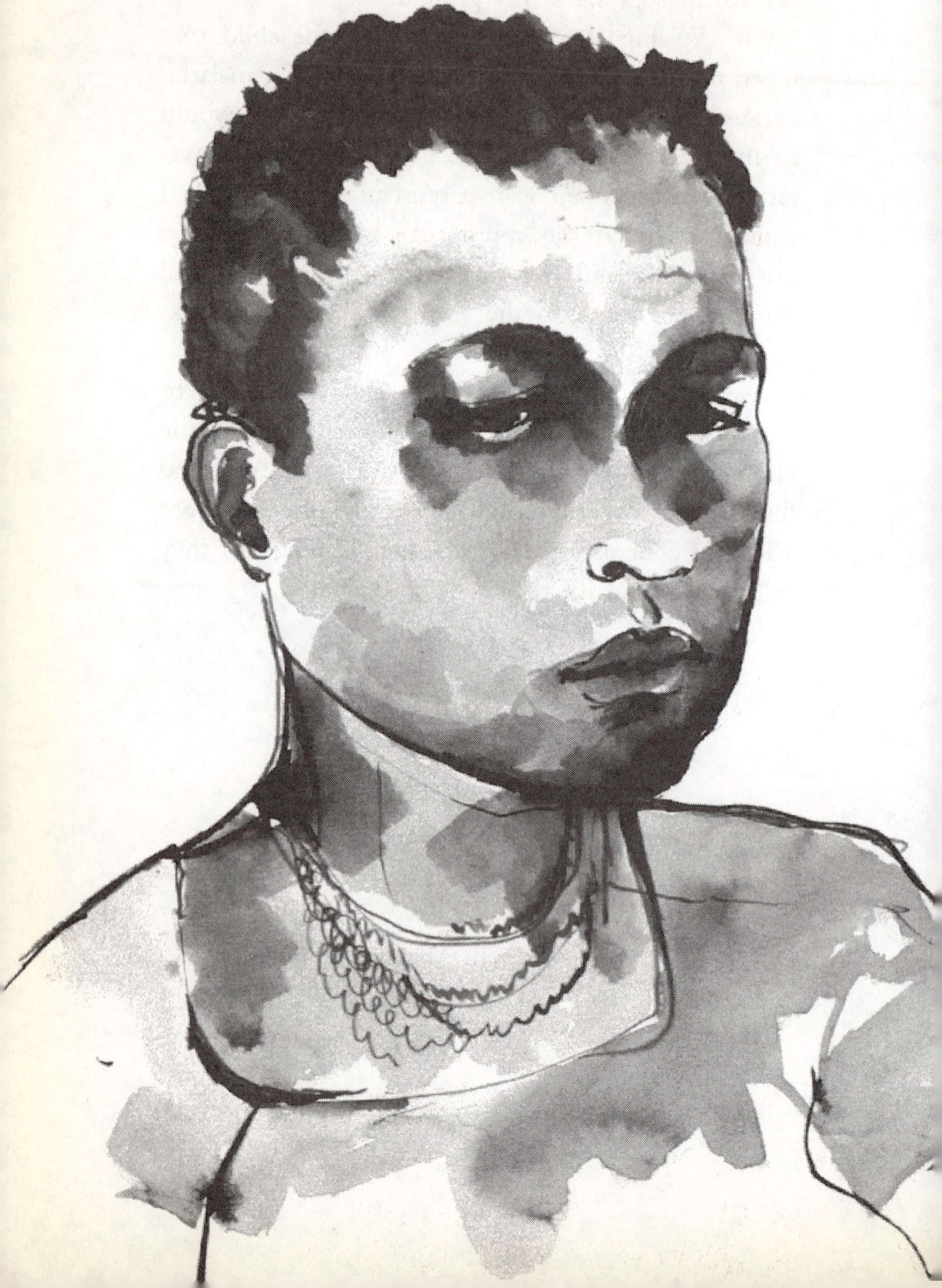

Tribes and Tribulations

7 November

This morning, as we were sitting having our morning coffee, we heard new sounds coming down the mountain—rhythmic, aggressive, chanting. We craned our necks, trying to see what was coming, and all the time the chants were getting closer, louder, more insistent. '*Whoo-oo, tst, tst, tst.*' And then we spotted them, through a gap in the trees, surging down the winding mountain road, running, stopping, running forward again, keeping time to their own war cries.

A small band of warriors going to battle. They had black cassowary plumes on their heads and charcoal on their faces. Their calls were the cries of death, and the few people huddled around our hut trembled with fear as the ancient war chant revived childhood memories of decimated houses and slaughtered relations. I could scarcely believe they were real, let alone terrifying. But the fear on the faces of Numndi and Pella told its own story. Numndi said that their blackened faces were a disguise used only for war.

'You can't kill a man whose face you know in cold blood,' he explained. 'The charcoal is the disguise which masks the man and makes him the enemy.'

Like a medieval suit of armour, I thought.

Even as we listened to our radio report on the latest neutron bomb, this archaic battalion was prancing quickly down past our hut, the front warrior rushing out in advance as the others brandished their spears, pretending to aim at him. If only we had had warning. I didn't even have time to load the camera. They were gone as soon as they came, where to, we did not yet know. Mishka and Jan followed them down the hill with the tape recorder, trying to record the sounds of their war cries.

We soon found out who they were and what was their cause. It was the Tipeka tribe, from up the mountain, going to war with the Palge tribe who inhabit the forested mountains on the other side of our valley. Their cause for revenge was the death of two of their clanswomen, whom, they claim, died from poisoning incurred at the hands of the Palge, their husbands' tribe. Death here, if not by accident, is usually attributed to ill will rather than natural causes, except in the cases of the very elderly.

11 November—Jan's thirteenth birthday

A propitious day, Armistice Day. The end of the First World War. A few bad things happened too: Ned Kelly the famous bushranger was hanged; Gough Whitlam our Prime Minister was betrayed; and now, here, a tribal war rages.

But for me this date will always evoke the sunny day in Crookwell when another little artist came into the world, right on 11.00 a.m. I saw his long artistic fingers and cried because I knew what he would become. We called him Jan.

Now it's his birthday and I'm wondering what entertainment I can provide for one who is such a young creator. 'Why don't you all go and watch the tribal war, while I fix the party feast?' I suggest to them.

They go off down the track. I sneak into my studio, slightly guilty that I should be indulging myself on my son's birthday. I've given Numndi some money to buy a duck from Brother Paul's mission farm and *mu-mu* it for the dinner. *Mu-mus* never fail to provide excitement, and there is a break in the bad weather which should definitely be enjoyed. Besides which, this means I have a few hours to myself, to paint.

Once again, in the evening, the *mu-mu* plus a train cake, a bit weird this time without Jan's strict style guidelines; far too much icing. But the cake and the chant provide wonderful entertainment—a combination of our ritual and theirs. Numndi can now sing the tune 'Happy Birthday'.

15 November

Every day now these warriors come at the same time and stand, shouting and brandishing their spears, at the base of the Palge mountain. The Palge wisely keep to the cover of their own territory. The warmongers then straggle back again in the late afternoon, for fighting down here conforms to strict rules: not before dawn, not in the heat of the noon-day sun and not after dark. How polite, I think. How terribly civilised.

The boys have amended their little tribal war game figures to look more like the real thing. Now the warriors have blackened faces and cassowary plumes, and they carry spears as well as shields.

17 November

Today as we 'watched the war', one of the dancing warriors spotted a pig running past. With a swift throw of his axe he just split the pig—an enemy pig—asunder. It made us feel sick, and suddenly very scared. I won't go and watch the war again. Nor will I urge the children 'Just go and watch the war will you!' I had begun to think it was more of a pantomime than a killing field. How wrong I was.

4 December

By the end of the war, which had lasted for weeks, all of the Palge houses that had been down in Rulna to be closer to the mission had been wrecked and the gardens devastated. Pigs had been killed, but there had been only minor injuries to people. The compensation claims on both sides were expedited by the sudden and somewhat amazing arrival of a member of parliament, clad in gleaming white, who descended from the skies in a green and white helicopter.

Helicopters never come here, so by the time it landed, with a great roar of wind, hundreds of forest dwellers had run out of the bush onto the cleared space. There was a huge crowd, including us, when the MP fired several shots into the air from a large gun.

After that the fighting stopped and so did all animosities. Compensation was settled. The Palge tribe had to promise to hand over several pigs, a large sum of money and two cassowaries. The helicopter left as dramatically as it had arrived, disappearing over the mountain wall of the valley.

The Palge emerged from their forested mountain and started visiting Rulna again. A Palge woman married to a Gamegai reappeared, walking down the road. At the outbreak of hostilities, we had been persuaded to drive this woman, hidden on the floor of the Toyota, through hostile Tipeka country to Hagen, where she remained for the duration of the war. This trip was, fortunately, landslide-free, because during wartime enemy women are raped, and God knows what they do to collaborators.

5 December

The wet season is full of storms—crashing, spectacular storms—and there are always tales of people or pigs getting struck down by lightning. Jonny, the mission store boy's mother, was struck the other day while walking along a mountain ridge. She is now paralysed in the Hagen hospital. This has added to my store of secret fears. When the children are away in the bush and I see a storm coming, I always think they will be struck. Today I was very happy to see them all straggling up towards the house, after the skies and surrounding mountains had been shaken by a great storm. Rafal was with Pella, snugly asleep in the bottom of her *bilum*. They were all there. I counted them as they came.

I have tried to carry Rafal in a *bilum*, like Pella does, encouraged and tutored by my women friends, but he doesn't like it at all coming from me. He becomes outraged at my attempts, immediately leaping up and demanding to be carried European style.

Still, I do carry my loads now in a head *bilum*. I was self-conscious at first, but it is very convenient and not as heavy as it looks. Nadya is much more agile and adept at this. Refusing to wear shoes, she has developed huge, splayed toes and angles her feet in the same way as the women here to give better mud grip. In vain I tell her that the sort of legs and feet she is developing here will not be at all desirable when we 'go back home'. She is scornful of my observations and scathingly retorts that her home is here now.

'And what about hookworm, Nadya!'

But she is gone before the words are even formed.

6 December
Dear Babcia

It's ages since I've written. I've been a negligent daughter-in-law and I'm sorry because you must worry about us. But there's no need to. Just think about Olek, that he was here in this place. People remember him, do you know that? Could you please send some of the photos of him doing the patrol? They want to see themselves in the photos.

Mishka and Jan seem to have retained their original identity; Nadya is a bit wilder, as you can probably imagine. But she is healthy, happy, and I keep a very good eye on her, so don't worry about her more than you have to. Olek is also keeping watch, as you know he would if he could. Well here, I believe, he can. I can really feel that. The boys fiddle about with the kids here, making targets for their bows and arrows, weaving mats. Jan makes tiny ornamental shields with identical markings to the real ones, mixing the ochres and dyes.

When the two boys have one of their famous arguments, Numndi and Ruminj, their two 'uncles', swagger in and separate them, taking a boy each on a hefty shoulder, and the crowd stands around, doubled with laughter. I don't have to say a thing. Here we don't see children fighting each other, only Jan and Mishka. Anyway, everybody loves it for the entertainment value.

Later . . .

Now is the time for the big *sing sing* around the pig exchange, the *moka*. This time it is the Tipeka, the tribe up the hill who have recently been at war, who are giving pigs to our tribe, the Gamegai. So each morning there is a mad rush for decoration.

Our house has mysteriously become a source of feathers, which are the main decoration for any festival. Numndi, Ruminj and Dokta, another new relative, pride themselves on having created a secure 'drying place' for the feathered bird corpses. We were searching for the source of a horrible smell, and then I found them, stuck into our ceiling on wooden stakes, two birds of paradise and one parrot. Jan and Mishka begged Numndi to dress them up too, pointing out that they'd had to put up with the stink so they deserved a bit of fun too.

So there they were, our boys, swaying among the lines of men, learning how to beat the long, waisted wooden drum called the *kundu*. Numndi and Pella were satisfied, and Kints, the 'grandfather', went along the line giving his nod of approval, like an old general taking the salute. I can imagine Olek looking at them too, with tears of pride in his eyes. I know that you are not an admirer of these sorts of cultures, but today even you would have enjoyed watching.

Nadya has become a teenager here in Rulna, a bit of a mother's nightmare and for sure a grandmother's as well. She is, as I suspected, now in love with Agena, a handsome sixteen-year-old whom she admires because he fed our pet bird. Well, perhaps he's fourteen too, but who would know? Agena has been persuaded by Jan to build a cookhouse to shelter an old iron stove that Brother Paul gave him to bake his bread in, and he is happy to do this as long as Nadya giggles and frolics somewhere around. Don't worry, she won't be in love with him forever, she's really quite fickle with her affections. I'll bring her back and we'll find a good Jewish boy for her.

They all play around while they build. Nadya fits in well here—her sense of fun being more or less the same as her new brothers' and sisters'. Every incident is considered funny. They drop one of the cross-planks and then double up with laughter. The construction of the cookhouse is a slow process. And Nadya is part of the reason for its slowness.

She struggles everywhere under a head *bilum*, her bare feet becoming as broad as the ferry boats on Sydney Harbour. Don't bother to buy any more dainty shoes for her for awhile. But could you please send us some t-shirts for the children?

And chocolate? Thanks for the last parcel, and for the little bear for Rafal. Kisses to you, and don't worry, we'll be back in one piece. I know you don't believe in Christmas but I hope yours is not lonely. We're thinking of you. You will probably go to Mum and Dad. If you do, take this letter and read it to them. Meanwhile, love to you from all of us.

Kathy

Nadya does preoccupy me, and more than just a bit. I think about the nights she spends at Numndi's house, curled up cosily with Pella and her children down the pigs' end of the hut. No doubt Agena sleeps there too, and would be aware of her presence as he sleeps down the men's end.

Men and women are strictly segregated. And the cunning Numndi can be completely trusted as a chaperone—I hope. Numndi's confident and persuasive manner engenders trust in me. But then I am becoming more and more aware that Numndi is a person with his own agenda.

Uncomfortably I start to wonder about who would actually score the pigs if Numndi managed to matchmake Nadya. Could it be that Numndi would get them? Is he not, in his words, their 'Rulna Papa'? Anyway, what would we do with pigs? Have we not got enough problems? And Numndi knows that. He knows I don't care for pigs.

22 December

Gris has given Mishka a *kapul*, an elegant black and white striped creature resembling a possum, the long tail of which, they warn Mishka, is coveted by the men here as a neck decoration. And there do seem to be hungry eyes on the helpless infant as it hangs imprisoned in a net bag in the house, or else sits prettily on Mishka's shoulder, dangling its prized tail down his chest. He calls it Malu Malu, the same as the pidgin for 'soft' and 'mud'.

In the meantime, another extraordinary drama has been unfolding. Pella's younger sister Moni, Nadya's friend, is a sultry beauty. She often accompanies Numndi when she is in Rulna and they appear to have an intimacy which is unusual between the sexes.

Now she has gone back to Tigi, where her parents live. They are part of the friendly Kawelka tribe, but now they don't seem very friendly to me as they have dragged Moni back up there entirely against her will. The cause? Moni had suddenly cut off her finger at the knuckle, supposedly as a protest against Numndi for calling her a loose flirt.

Many older men and women here have hands which bear such signs of past mutilation. We were told that they used to sever their own fingers from the knuckle as a sign of mourning for a lost family member. Moni's case, however, has shocked us. She is so young, so beautiful. Her desperate act seems incomprehensible, even, I'm thankful to note, to Nadya. She has become so Gamegarised that I would not have put it past her to perform such an act if it occurred to her that it was necessary.

Now, astonishingly, Moni's relations want her to give them K300 (that's about A$400) as compensation for her injury, which they see as their loss in terms of her diminished marketability as a bride. With a hewn-off finger, they say, Moni will fetch a lesser brideprice.

They claim, in addition, that Numndi has been having his way with her. He was outraged. He asked her to bare her belly, gesturing dramatically to indicate to them her non-pregnant state. Moni obliged, surly expression intact. Pella remained impassive throughout, her feelings unknown. Her face was hidden as she concentrated on weaving a *bilum*, rubbing and rolling the strands of bush string on her thigh and intricately hooking them along the row, like fast crochet. Moni was escorted back to Tigi.

So here we are, three days before Christmas. We have already been here nine months. We have guests coming: Maryla from Poland and Tony from the Sepik. We have dragged everything out into the sun and washed and swept and tidied. It doesn't feel like Christmas. Our Christmas tree, a small pawpaw tree growing outside our hut, has already been stripped of its festive baubles, after one night. It has ceased to be a Christmas tree and is now a mere tree again.

3 January

Many things have happened to us over the past fortnight. Our visitors arrived. The *moka*, starting off like a murmur with a few decorated and almost unobserved performer-donors beating their *kundu* drums and 'dancing', has gradually worked its way up into a huge crescendo. Each day there are more participants dancing and chanting, more feathers being swapped, borrowed, stolen.

The atmosphere has become frenetic as each morning the men, having decided who among them deserves the decorations for the day, 'make-up' in small mirrors all around our house. The Toyota mirror is a favourite. Otherwise small fragments of mirror will serve the purpose of monitoring the elaborate face-painting procedure. In this area the predominant colours are black, white and red.

My paints and the feathers and *kina* shells the boys have collected are in demand, but it seems that our Christmas tinsel is the most coveted, and is now being worn as proudly as any feathers. Our Christmas tree glitters and twinkles on a sea of festooned heads.

Our visitors have announced that the reason for their visit is that they want to marry, and they need Voytek to give the bride away and to be the witness. Maryla Wronska is an old friend of Voy's from Poland, an anthropologist, and her fiancé, Tony Friend, is an English patrol officer who lives in the Western Province.

We had a mad drive to the Bishop's house in Mount Hagen early in the morning, hoping that he could waive all the documents needed for the marriage because Poland is under martial law and Maryla's are trapped inside her beleaguered homeland. Bishop Bernadin, a corpulent veteran of this mission business from San Francisco, gave permission without bothering to change out of his bedroom slippers and dressing-gown. He was chewing cough lollies, one after the other, from a big bag, as he perused the documents before signing. He certainly did not look like a bishop. But the task was done.

Then the car broke down and we had to stay with a friend, Alice Hohnen, in Hagen until it was fixed. We could not stay at the hostel because Malu Malu, the *kapul*, had travelled with us on Mishka's shoulder.

Mishka's *kapul* was not a good houseguest. He kept escaping at night, charging around the house, entering all the rooms like Houdini, uttering nocturnal screeches and glaring furiously with his luminous red eyes from the tops of cupboards. And our hostess was not marsupially inclined.

Voy's and my furious (and ingenious) attempts to trap Malu Malu in various barricaded corners in the middle of the night were to no avail. He outwitted us every time, reappearing with renewed enthusiasm, dashing about the ceiling and screeching his marsupial messages, keeping the whole weary household wide awake. All, that is, except Mishka, his keeper, who refused to believe our tales of the night's outrage. I didn't tell Mishka that Voy had at one stage suggested flushing the offending pet down the toilet.

We got back for New Year's Eve. We rejoined the

moka, the boys and Nadya dancing in circles—arms entwined, hair flopping, sweating, never stopping—me recording and Voy taking photos.

The evening was spent quietly at the mission. 'Boring,' said Nadya. We got up early on New Year's Day to prepare for the wedding, putting flowers round the house, clearing away all traces of rotten pawpaws and bananas, cleaning the floor and the tables and placing candles in beer bottles.

The wedding was to be at 11.00 a.m., so off we went to make sure Father Josef was there. But the frenetic buzz of the *moka* in the air was to override all our arrangements. There could be no mass, no wedding while the dancing was on. There would be no-one to sing, no-one to serve the mass, no-one to attend. All the potential wedding guests were feathered, painted and fully occupied. What could we do but go along with them and arrange once again to have the ceremony in the evening or when the dancing ceased?

The bride would have to wash in the river once again as her white dress was now smeared with pig grease and sweat. Lines of Tipeka men, handsome and shining in their black, white and red face-paint and full headdress, were swaying and dipping, stamping to the rhythm of the *kundu* drums. Our Gamegai tribesmen were in circles, arm over shoulder, *k-lapping* and singing, with women in their own circles. From time to time they would parade in a long line in front of the drum-beating Tipeka. Voy was rushing around with his zoom lens and I was wandering and sketching, having deposited Rafal with a group of women seated in the shade.

As the *sing sing* drew to a close, our young lovers appeared, walking solemnly down the track, flowers in hand, dressed in white wedding clothes. We dressed ourselves very seriously. Dokta Miki looked the best with his coloured highland two-corner hat, white doctor's coat and black and white *kapul* seated proudly on his shoulder.

The tiny church was full of men with paint and headdress, and the evening closed down over the service, ending in a crash of thunder, lightning which seemed to zigzag through the frail building, and a mighty downpour. We all struggled through the mud and the rain up the valley to our place, where we lit the candles, preparing for the feast to be brought in.

The champagne, delicious pork on outspread banana leaves, and the sight of the painted faces, grotesque in the lamplight, suspended in the shadows around the feast, made a bizarre wedding reception. There was loud singing, first them and then us, going far into the night.

Ruminj and Numndi were teaching the children *tanim het* to a chorus of raucous laughter when suddenly the little hut was shaken by flashes of lightning and the crash, bang, crack of thunder; we sat quietly, silenced by the greater forces.

So, Saturday came, the last day of the *moka*. The heat was intense, as were the make-up preparations in the morning. Our wedding guests had stayed the night after the wedding, being unwilling to undertake the long trek home to their distant houses at night in the rain. How quickly they adjust to our soft ways. They all made beds for themselves, knowing exactly what we had to spare in the way of bedding, and argued between themselves about who would sleep on what. Early the next morning, with the first streak of pink sky over the mountains, the bits of chipped mirror were out and the painting had started.

The last day of the *moka* is the most exciting. Just as the pigs are brought down again, painted with clay, the *olga*—the extra 'surprise'—is presented, and then the decorated pigs are chased squealing from the bush, pursued by men and women with spears.

5 January

A giant pig feast was prepared for the Tigi tribe just through the bush at the back of our house, a traditional *mu-mu* place. It seemed to be on a larger scale than any we had seen in this spot, and I wanted to really learn the many stages of the *mu-mu*: the killing of the pigs, the expert quartering with bamboo knives, the heating of the stones, and the lining of the holes in the ground with banana leaves. The raw pork and the hot stones are lowered deftly into the steaming holes with bamboo tongs, the sweet potatoes and green vegetables are all sealed off and cooked together, producing a certain aroma, and then everything is lifted out and ceremoniously shared.

Mishka must be considered a bit of an expert now, because he was allowed to help and was rewarded with a bit of dripping pork. He dangled it in his fingers until I insisted that he cook it, together with the other children's meat, which they had started to barbecue on the fire. Fruitlessly, I grumbled on about the dangers of *pig-bel*, the endemic and fatal pig poisoning feared in the highlands after feasts. At the end of the *mu-mu* they all moved to the old *moka* ground, transporting the pork on huge banana leaves, and one man shouted out the names of people to come and receive it; *bik-mousing*, it is called here. Each person received their portion in order of importance, which was calculated according to size and cut. The women, I noticed, received the entrails. Rulna is hardly a feminist stronghold.

Voytek is rushing everywhere. Some Jimmi men have appeared and he is keen to talk to them about why they are here. At the same time he wants to watch the pig feast and check on the protocol and rituals. Our people are afraid of the Jimmi people whom they consider to be evil and magic.

It's a late night and there's too much talk, too much activity. I am tired and am going to flop without even forcing lazy Mishka to wash and clean his teeth. What's the point, anyway? It is survival, not elegance and hygiene at this stage. Our clothes are mere rags and our feet are permanently ingrained with mud. I have no underpants left at all and my only surviving footwear is a huge pair of gumboots, as muddy on the inside as they are on the outside.

6 January

Today must be the sixth. Voy has gone to a meeting with Father Josef and the men from the Jimmi. Nadya and Jan are washing the clothes in the swollen river. They still take hours to do it, even though their swimming activities have been curtailed by the unfriendly water.

I have to try to resurrect a few 'respectables' for the children's forthcoming Australian tour. The trip will be a health cure, to rid Jan of some sort of asthma he's picked up and Nadya of her ulcers, and so the skinny boys can put on a little weight to prepare for the few months ahead.

7 January

Our three chooks have been stolen and, the evidence says, slain by an enemy tribe. The remains of the feast have been discovered in a cave up on the mountain, and Numndi and Ruminj are anxious to clear up the matter in the High Court at Moglam, which settles inter-tribal disputes. They feel that they know the identity of the thieves. The invigorating thought of compensation is in the air. But the prospect of a long-winded court session at uncomfortable Moglam, and the possibility of being presented with three kina, a cassowary in a cage or a squealing pig to bring back in the car at the end of the session does not interest me. Voytek, his anthropological curiosity dampened by my refusal to cooperate, has agreed to drop the matter. Disappointment reigns.

Mickey's *kapul* has chosen parmesan cheese as his primary nourishment. He disappears into the cardboard tube containing the cheese, and only his black and white tail remains visible while he feeds. I hope for our sakes he does not develop a stomach upset. Rafal has diarrhoea again. It's a semi-permanent state with him but it does not stop his dogged attempts to walk, climb and raid the scrap bucket, in a similar fashion to the way the *kapul* approaches the parmesan. His walk is heavily assisted by any object, real or imaginary, within grasp.

The Tigi tribe has come and gone, together with their local officials, ex-Councillor Kuk and present Councillor Kongga. These two men are rivals. Neither can stand the other, which causes tension when both are crowded into our little room, a favoured meeting place. Kongga is smooth and boasts about his primary education. Kuk is appealing and bear-like, but is permanently out of sorts now that he's lost his position of councillor to Kongga. He refuses, however, to surrender his badge of office. 'Never' he says, and this puts Kongga under a lot of strain. Very male behaviour, I can't help thinking.

17 January

Sunday. The children have gone to Australia for three weeks. They are missed. The place is quiet. Voy is in one of his grouches and I'm refusing to make the effort needed to get him out of it. We have been sparring for a couple of days now, aiming private verbal daggers at each other despite the ever-present company. The tension is unbearable and everybody feels it. How did it start anyway? For me it is impossible to see any correlation between the sort of minor irritation which initially besets him and the dark mood which then completely engulfs him, shutting me out, making me the enemy. His eyes, normally twinkly and inviting, become cold blue pinpoints. Needles of ice. His bulky, sheltering body becomes a hostile mound, enemy territory, not to be trespassed upon. His normal affectionate chitchat turns into caustic and heavily barbed remarks.

Pushed out of my warm paradise, I try to cajole my way back, but then, just as I am on the point of gaining ground, I somehow lose patience and reach for my own ammunition, hurling at him everything I can dredge up, all the way. And Voy, on the point of negotiating a peace, retreats again to his defences as my final insults begin to find their inner target. I run for cover, trying then to recall the ammunition; but the damage is done.

It has been two days of mental torture, existing without nourishment, without communication, irritable and cross with everyone, tired from sleepless nights listening to the rats in their playground above our heads, furious with the fact that Voy can actually sleep soundly, his back turned against me, leaving me in my distressed state—he who has after all been the cause of this distress. Rafal cries and I fetch him, thankful for the little warm body, loving and uncritical, needing his night fears soothed. Together we drift into sleep, his face snuffling into my neck, his curls under my hand.

The morning reminds me again that I am in the war zone and peace is not in sight. Numndi worries and constantly chides us; Pella just giggles her deep giggle. Kints and Numndi try to bring us together using their highly developed peacemaking skills. Once, they nearly succeeded. Voy almost laughed—I caught it in his eyes—but he stopped just in time, retaining, with effort, his impenetrable brooding demeanour.

I had to escape. But where to? With the mountain behind, the forests to the side and the river in front, it was not easy to leave my little war zone. Nevertheless I grabbed Rafal, heavy by now, and put him in his backpack. Then I went up to the top of Mt Winimp, to the presentation of the brideprice for Dokta.

This is where Voy should be, with me, celebrating. Dokta is his friend! My resentment began to simmer again as I contrasted my fully righteous position with his embittered negativity. And then I became distracted by the activity around me.

Dokta's new wife's 'line' was there, down from Tigi. Having given over the young bride, they were waiting to receive their pigs, which were duly dragged up the track, one by one, screaming and struggling against their uncertain fate. Kints, Dokta's father, was angrily chiding his sons because not enough pigs had been brought. At least that seemed to be a good enough explanation to offer me when I asked why Kints, usually reticent and benign, was looking and sounding so fierce.

We sat around in the mud for several hours and the men gossiped and worried about pigs, and the women prepared the firewood for the marita *mu-mu* where the pandanas fruit is cooked in a ground oven. Ruminj's eventual arrival with his pig was greeted with evident relief, and I reclaimed my sweaty baby, put him on my back and struggled home down the track, slipping and floundering at times in the deep mud and delicately picking my way across the river by jumping from boulder to boulder.

When we got home we found the house surrounded by a crowd of people all suing the girl Maria for stealing Meta's bra, which, they claimed, Meta had been given by Nadya. Once again, the bra being displayed did not look like any I had ever bought for Nadya. It was the pink, heavily padded nursing bra type, rather grubby and designed for watermelon breasts. There was a feeling of deja-vu about the whole matter. And why was it being conducted around our house, anyway?

My resilience had deserted me, leaving me sensitive and petulant. I was not prepared for this gross invasion of privacy, leaving us no spot in which to carry out our daytime existence other than the dark confines of the hut. Anyway, what use was privacy, when Voy was in this stink? I ignored him, as he continued to ignore me, and I left again, stalking off to the river. I was struggling to hold back tears because I did not want anyone to see me crying, especially Voy. Why should he have that satisfaction?

The river felt cool and fresh, invigorating and relaxing, making my skin feel silky, washing away my tension and anger along with the dirt and sweat and pig smells. We lay a little on the warm rocks. Rafal looked clean and glowing again. When he gets dirty, which is all the time, his white skin offsets the layers of grime and sweat, and he looks like a beggar's baby.

19 January

I spent another uneasy night sleeping beside my estranged husband in a little hut in the middle of the darkest jungle in the world. We were woken early to go 'on top' to Kay's house, where a funeral feast was underway. Up we went, higher and higher. They kept saying '*Klos tu*' and I knew it wasn't. Across creeks and rocks, through sloshy swamps we struggled, up steep slopes and past high gardens, up and up again. And still further. One more hour.

Then there we were. The cool breeze fanned our hot faces as we stood, gasping, staring down at the amazing view beneath us. Next to us, on the ground, was the funeral feast, a line of cooked pigs, stacked neatly and waiting for the distribution ceremony. The last thing I felt like consuming was slightly cooked pork. Nevertheless, Voy was still maintaining a level of fury even after all those hours of climbing, and the sight of him hissing at me threateningly made me graciously accept the treat. We did, however, make a tacit agreement to wrap our share in a banana leaf to carry it home, so that the flyblown looking morsel could at least be recooked and our consumption of it rather more optional than public.

On the way back I became so hot I took one of Rafal's wet nappies and put it on my head, like a veil, to cool me against the sun. And then, in the middle of a patch of grass, I sat down just where I was and refused to move. Meri Ko sat with me, my silent supporter. And Voytek, not exhausted at all but choosing not to proceed without me, kept snapping his camera at me and my nappy hat. I just sat, drained of response, too hot for resentment, waiting to regain the energy needed for the furious plunge down the steep path.

Just before we arrived home, clutching our huge backsides of pork, Gris hurt his leg, chopping it open with his axe while cutting firewood for us. Blood spurted everywhere and he lay back, eyes shut, moaning ominously, with various bits of bush attached and twisted as tourniquets around his leg.

Dokta Miki, why aren't you here? Where's my first aid kit? What does the book say: 'Raise the leg and apply pressure, stop the bleeding'? Eventually we found a *dokta boy* and happily committed the patient to his care. By this time his mother had been summoned by the yodelling system used here, which involves shouting messages from mountain top to mountain top. She started to wail and tear her hair at his side in a disconcerting fashion, making the emergency even worse than it already was.

20 January

Voy and I are basking in a divine truce. Calm and confident with each other, it is difficult to even remember how bad it was. Hostilities were impossible to sustain, even for Voytek, a master of the siege. He, to commemorate the peacemaking, prepared a special dinner: chicken with tinned Chinese sauce and tinned soup. It doesn't sound great, but the occasion made it delicious.

We had decided to honour Ruminj and Kints with the gift of our pork backsides. Our relief at giving equalled their sheer joy in receiving—a gift that suited both the donors and the recipients. This had forced me and Voy into sly collaboration, but, making a huge effort with the last of my energy, I resisted making the next move at reconciliation and left the initiative to him, having to trust that he would take it.

For the chicken dinner he even produced a bottle of wine from under a heap of clothes—all part of the great thaw. We lit a candle and were able to talk. He was feeling stupid, worried about work, about writing, about time passing and about not having enough English words. He had slumped, feeling only despair and aggression. It hadn't been my fault after all. Well, if he had told me that in the beginning it would have prevented a lot of suffering and saved me from hurling all those stupid insults. Too late. They will no doubt be remembered and reactivated at a later date, but for now we are safe, and very glad to have found each other.

Today was a fine day, and from the early morning we could hear *bik-mousing* all over the hills, calling men from the three tribes living on their three different mountains to work on the broken bridge across the Winimp River. The Gamegais had already gathered and were trudging up the hill, but the Palge didn't come, nor the Mabege, so the work was called off.

The Palge did surface later, however; not to fix the bridge, but to sue Anis, a Gamegai who had been *greasing* (seducing, or attempting to seduce) one of their married women. After prolonged discussion, the compensation was fixed at two pigs—one for K300 and one for K200—to be paid by Anis (or, as is the custom here, Anis's clan) not to the woman but to the cuckolded husband. I'm not sure to what extent he was *greasing* her; he claimed not at all. They said the look on his face in court proved him guilty, but Anis *always* has that look.

The defendant can actually be exonerated here,

despite hard evidence, if he can sustain a look of outraged innocence during the trial. Perhaps it's not all that different to back home, when the young defendant is prepared to cut and brush his hair and even betray his belief system and put on a suit in order to sway the mind of the magistrate.

Today, too, I bought two beautiful *bilums* made by Gris's sister and sister-in-law. They came to the house asking if I wanted to buy them and I jumped at the offer. The beautiful deep baby *bilums*, never destined to carry lowly sweet potato and taro, are woven intermittently with dashes of red and stripes of the *kus kus* fur from the possum. When I gave them seventy kina they carefully laid it out on the ground, counting it slowly, again and again.

Voytek is getting stale and feels like going away somewhere for a few days break. He feels imprisoned by the place, by the people, and admits to feeling bored with pigs. Already he has been here for fourteen months. I try to reassure and encourage him, reason with him. 'Look, Voy! This society must be pretty close to Utopia! Look, they sit and talk and laugh and walk, they go bush just to find a few feathers or a bit of bark for a belt. They're public about their suspicions. And the ancestors all help out. We're doing well here! We're learning! Don't start getting down on the place now!'

It's true, we are learning something, something about life. Quite a lot, in fact. We have seen here that death is as familiar as birth, and reaction to death is predictable and ritualised. It is reassuring because it seems to be part of the cycle of life. Back home, birth is hospitalised and death is an alien concept, managed by death professionals and with a variety of existing funeral rites and customs at our disposal. Nobody really deals with it. By physically separating ourselves from birth and death, we have deprived ourselves of the ability to appreciate their meaning.

The same with conflict and its resolution. Fighting is a dirty word back home. Frowned upon. Only 'foreigners' do it. It's almost better to suffer the tension and the insult forever than to speak out. Good friendships, work relationships, marriages are ruined because it is considered better to shut up and say nothing than to risk losing everything; festering is permitted, but not direct outlets. Here a man can take his brother to court in the morning and eat and joke with him in the afternoon. Mikel Kewa's wife tore all his *dokta boy*'s clothes to shreds because he was spending too much time with Berum, his second wife. That was only last week, when the furious husband came beseeching us to take his first wife, Maria, away in our car as far as we could, and just leave her there. He showed us the remains of a once-proud white uniform. Now they have made up and are the best of friends again, even though Mikel Kewa has no white uniform and has to wear his bush greens.

'And yet,' says Voy pessimistically, 'as we watch them, like dream people in a paradise, they are about to be doomed, Kot.' Voytek is such a pessimistic Slav, it is an automatic reaction with me to remain unmoved by his gloomy predictions. I want to think of Rulna as it is forever. But his words keep nagging me. 'The lure of our Western ways will come here as they do everywhere, Kot, bringing chaos and confusion, moral and physical poverty.'

22 January

Peter Kewa, Ruminj's grown-up stepson, is one of the local *dokta boys* who has been selected to go to nursing school. He is afraid to leave, to travel to places where he has no relations. He says that he will surely be killed in the bus. We have outfitted him with clothes for the cold Enga province.

The family has collected money for him and yet at the last moment he will probably be too terrified to leave. Not only is he convinced his 'enemies' (non-tribe-members) will get him, but his brothers reinforce his fears. There has been a discussion and they have asked Voytek to go with Kewa to Enga. The duties of an anthropologist are nothing if not diverse; now he is a protector against enemy tribes.

24 January

Kabuga, our cat, has had another four kittens and we don't know what to do about her regular reproduction. There are no vets around here to do 'the operation'. Malu Malu the pet *kapul* is alive and well.

Last night we were woken by the droning sounds of men singing *tanim het* songs as they courted the girl in the old ritual, the girl sitting demurely in front of the fire, hands on lap, her suitors swaying in turn or in duet beside her, rubbing noses with her, twisting up and down, their tall head feathers sweeping the ground. Again and again, over and over, far into the night.

We lay there wondering whether to go out or not, tempted by the songs yet warm in bed. It must have been two in the morning when we went, picking our way up the path towards the sound. The moon was so bright there was no need for a lamp. I noticed that we even cast moonshadows.

We had Rafal wrapped and asleep in his blanket, following the sounds as they grew gradually louder. Then we came to the hut and crept in, trying not to disturb the romantic tension of the solemn ceremony. Huddled at the back, we watched once again, mesmerised by the droning songs directed at the couple by the hearth. And then we walked back again as the light of the red dawn broke the grey over the mountain ridges.

25 January

I have spent hours talking with Voy about his work, about his trouble with English. All his field notes are written in a mixture of Polish and pidgin and some

English. He has a huge dictionary here and writes lists of English words, memorising them. He knows many more words than I do but he uses them in such an unusual way that I fail to recognise what he is trying to say, and he gets upset with me. He tries to explain to me about his conversations with Dokta, about everything here, how it must have evolved like this, how Christianity is perceived and transformed by local lore.

And now I've left him to his conversations with Dokta, who has just appeared, and gone back to my own work. My struggle to paint is always calling me, but I still allow myself to be pulled and distracted too easily. Rafal's sweet noises only have to change to a whimper and I put aside my tools and go for a cuddle, or the chooks decide to lay an egg on my papers, or a colourful and tumultuous crowd goes down the path, tempting me to follow. Today, however, I will not be waylaid.

I'm going to allow my mind to be swept by colours, shadows, light, forms. I'm nearly satisfied, learning to understand the nature of the paper and the watercolour and to get just the right amount of contrast—depth and strength, the incredible softness of the greys and the greens, the elusive and moving light. Once again I have been painting mothers and babies, expressing my own condition which links me to the women more strongly than words ever could. Babies are in their mothers' hands, hands made strong by years of work in their gardens. Babies are oblivious to their mothers' weariness, asleep or awake as they please or hungry and seeking those worn-out breasts once again.

I can hear the men laughing and joking, talking about girls. They keep singing fragments of the *tanim het* songs from the night before, and the maiden of the night, a member of the Kawelka tribe from Tigi, stands outside our *haus kuk*, her mysterious nocturnal splendour spent. She stands stolidly clad in lap-lap (loincloth or sarong) and heavy chokers of beads which do nothing to disguise her plump face and body. The men here like fat, they say *'gris* [fat] is beautiful, thin means old.' Looking around, it makes sense; there are no fat old men or women. They lose their fat very quickly, walking and climbing all those muddy, slippery miles every day to their houses which are scattered at wide and steep intervals throughout the mountains.

26 January

Last night we went to the mission—just a social visit, a whisky and a chat. It had been raining and dark all day and Rafal was sick. We left Pugga and Agena in charge of our house and our baby. Father Josef and Nimu, the recently imported volunteer bush nurse from India, were making tapestries. Enlivened by the female company, the young man seemed to be in better spirits than I'd seen him for a long time. He says the Jimmi trip is in ten days. I don't want to stay here alone without Voy, but the children will be back. Of course it would be the ideal opportunity to do some work.

Now we feel like a break. We are planning to take Peter Kewa to Hagen and put him on the bus to go to Enga. He is still terrified at the thought of nursing school, and it may be necessary to take half of his family to accompany him to the door of the hospital and then return. That will be our break.

Good day today, workwise. I forced myself to work out a semi-vision I have been obsessed with for ages—a small artistic puzzle, but over the months I've wasted pages and pages of valuable handmade paper, despairing over my failure to achieve a fine balance between subject, colour, draughtsmanship, and soft and sharp lines.

Voytek had a good day, too. He compares himself to a large plane, trembling with power and yet often unable to take off, just stuck on the runway. 'I feel like a *curva* Boeing, Kot—all jets firing but I'm *curva* stuck!' He always sprinkles his frustrated talk with *curva*. It means 'whore' in Polish, and he warns me and the children never to say the word in front of his aunties or any polite society in Poland. I think it's the only Polish word we know, by repetition.

But the *curva* plane is a good comparison for him. Today he took off, today and yesterday. He's in full flight, ideas and pen flowing, so we are both productive.

28 January

Malu Malu has disappeared. His *bilum* hangs empty. The nights are no longer accompanied by his noisy searches around the ceiling. The parmesan cheese remains uneaten. And Mishka, his keeper, is due back tomorrow. My desperate inquiries produce only sympathetic shrugs or a long list of suspects who may, according to Numndi, have had their eye on the tail as an ornament, to dangle smartly from a neckband and nestle between the rounded, glistening pectoral muscles of an elegant tribesman preparing for the *moka*.

6 February

The past few days have been a time of adjustment. The children are back, with a bang. Mishka, as I suspected he would, rushed straight into the hut, to check Malu Malu's bag. He emerged with a sad and knowing look in his eyes.

'You didn't look after him properly!'

What could I say? I didn't even like touching Malu Malu, Mishka knew that. I have an aversion to rodent-like creatures. But equally, I explained uselessly to Mishka, Malu Malu avoided me. Mishka became silent, not caring to fool himself about Malu Malu's fate.

7 February

We are expecting visitors: Francesca and Allan, anthropologist linguists who work in the upper Nebilya

Valley, and archaeologist Paul Gorecki. The rain is heavy and constant, the mud squelchy and thick, and I have had diarrhoea now for close on two weeks. I've forgotten what it's like to do a normal shit. All the native cures—ginger, pawpaw milk, pawpaw soup—have failed. (I've refused Pella's offer of *nuntz*, the nettle leaf cure.)

Well, time heals all, I guess. Meri Meta is now living with Nadya in her room and they giggle half the night and gossip about boys. Nadya has told us of Meta's predicament. 'I don't know who I love the more, Jesus Christ or Peter Kewa. It makes me so sad.' Nadya thinks that Peter Kewa is handsome enough to make the choice an easy one for Meta. In her shoes (or rather her bare feet), Jesus Christ being invisible and all that, Nadya would definitely go for Peter Kewa.

Dokta and Kongga, his new wife, had a big row tonight. It seems that he wants to take another wife, having just barely concluded his first marriage. Numndi is angry with him—probably jealous. Numndi, like all the men here, sees getting another wife as highly desirable. Not too many achieve their aim, because it is difficult to convince clansmen to fork out yet another set of pigs for someone who already has a wife when there are so many young men without women. But they still talk about it. And the first wife furiously resists the idea of a second wife.

Rafal still has no teeth and no sign of any, but he doesn't care, and his lack of teeth does not seem to prevent him from eating whatever he chooses. He tries to raid the scrap bucket. I usually catch him in time, and drag him screaming away from his prize goal, with its lid that snaps open when he treads on the pedal. He is suddenly extremely mobile, and this means constant vigilance.

Nadya at least is giving me a break. She has decided she doesn't like any boys here now, and not even Agena. We sometimes talk about home—family, friends, the garden, hot water and electricity, a weekend in Sydney, a day at the beach, a treat. Sometimes I don't feel like leaving here and at other times the thought of getting on that luxurious plane southward-bound makes me fantasise dangerously. Even the supermarket down the road, and our boring station wagon and bitumen roads assume exaggerated proportions in my dreams.

10 February

Malu Malu has returned. With his tail intact. He was brought to Mishka by a noisy delegation who claimed to have discovered the thief. Once again we were exhorted to take the offender to court. Once again we refused. It is enough that Mishka and Malu Malu are together again.

We've had our visitors. They stayed for two nights and now they've gone. It was fun, for a change, to talk to normal people—if you can call other anthropologists normal, which I doubt. But then perhaps we are not normal either, so that makes communication perfect.

Allan and Francesca left nauseous and ill, poor things. We wanted them to love staying with us, to keep them here for a bit and show the place to them. We were wondering what could have made them sick, and felt bad about it. Was it the food, the hygiene, the water? Paul Gorecki had his raincoat stolen, and he furiously summoned various local men, threatening repercussions if the garment was not returned.

13 February

Unlike the *kapul*, the coat never surfaced. And of course there were no repercussions. But Paul returned. He came back again two days later with an English professor of biology, Dick Morton. Dick is optimistic and garrulous, a veritable fountain of knowledge of all sorts, a good person to have here. We don't need any more depressive introverts.

Dick wanted to catch rats to take home, and to find bush turkey eggs. He and Paul marched off into the green distance this morning, taking some men with them as guides and leaving us in charge of catching the rodents. The boys, needless to say, were intrigued by such a challenge. They set Dick Morton's traps, laden with peanut butter, in all of the rat haunts.

Alas, in such a rat-infested hole not one single rat was caught. Nothing, however, dampened Dick Morton's jaunty mood. Each night he produced a bottle of rum, had a swig, offered us one, and returned it to his bag. By the end of the second night half a bottle was left. Our vain hopes that he would give us the remainder of the rum upon leaving were not rewarded. Dick and the rat traps and the rum departed intact. I'm glad he got no rats. They must have instinctively avoided his stupid peanut butter.

14 February

There is a big *sing sing* going on up the road and the participants prance past with their painted faces and their wives walking behind, the humble bearers of their husbands' plumage, pressed in flat bush splints and carried on their heads.

Voytek is preparing himself for the trek to the Jimmi and I am bracing myself, walling us in with enough food and medicines to withstand the time alone without a trip to town. It is raining heavily. Mud is a sea all around the house. Gumboots are lying everywhere and the clothes don't dry. The mattresses are mouldy and all leather has gone blue.

15 February

Nadya has started to do her schoolwork, which arouses my suspicions. What can she really be up to? I wonder, knowing that her interests usually lie elsewhere. Jan always works. Mishka... well, Mishka is

Mishka. He takes lots of photographs with an old-fashioned camera. He reads, plays, talks, he does his clinic. He is very busy. But he does not want to do his correspondence course.

The pleasant voice of his teacher comes out of the cassette, cajoling and offering assistance. And Mishka puts equally pleasant messages on the return tape, couched in eloquent language which defies his years. But he will not do his exercises. He would prefer to endure torture than subject himself to this small discipline. And short of applying torture, which is not really my forte anyway, all I can do is struggle with my own frustration at the no-win situation. Voy is less patient. Being Polish, he cannot see how a life can be successful if it lacks the constraints and rigours of a curriculum-based education. It makes us fight.

'But what about Einstein?' I offer, desperate not only to win a point with him, but somehow to convince myself. 'He failed at school and then he invented the atomic bomb!'

'So what that he invented a bomb? Do we want Mishka to invent a bomb? And how do you know about Einstein's school record? I bet, Kot, you don't know what energy equals, you expert on Einstein!'

Well, as a matter of fact I do know that energy equals MC squared, because I used to have a boss whose initials were MC and that made me remember. But I wisely got off the argument at this point, suspecting myself to be on shaky ground and not wanting to subject myself to any further worrying about my son who spurns his schoolwork.

I got two letters in the last mailbag, one from Mum and one from a friend, with three books. How wonderful it is to get a letter, that cosy, secret thing, reading the news and thoughts then reading it to Voy. And then, oh joy, another book to occupy the evening hours while Voy is working.

We try to read the same books and then talk about them and discuss all the ideas and why the author thought of them. Books transport us to other worlds, and then we return, with a sharp bang, to the realities of Rulna.

We have just trekked, all of us, up to Wei's house in Palge, the mountain beyond the valley and over the river. We had heard Wei was dying, and as he was the grand old bigman of Palge, we were advised that we should, in the manner of these people, 'pay homage'. We knew little about Wei, except that he had had eleven wives but six of them drowned after he threw them into the river in order to set some sort of example to the others.

Wei, upon our discreet and tentative entrance into the house of his deathbed, leapt up, greeted us enthusiastically, made several lengthy speeches and gave Voy two kina as a sign of friendship, which put us on his list of people for whom he has done favours. He then proceeded to wheel and deal in the manner of the bigmen here. He invited us to partake of the pigs which were being sacrificed on behalf of his illness, and then he attempted to persuade Voy to buy him some cartridges to keep in case of another war.

Weighed down with the last requests of a dying man, we struggled home—a long, slippery and muddy trek. I was getting tired, Mishka too. It took us seven hours altogether, up and down, across flooding rivers. We crept across one long, shaky, single sapling bridge on all fours, feeling and looking really cowardly but unwilling to risk our necks for the sake of our pride.

Nadya and Jan, in their usual ostentatious fashion, raced us home, streaking across the sapling bridges, defying the angry, snaking river below and defying my protests as I thought of Wei's drowned wives.

16 February

Once again I have been cleaning, sewing and reorganising to make the place pretty and comfortable for a visitor. We have had good news. Becky, a friend of Kate, is coming for six weeks, a fresh school-leaver from London. She is going to act as tutor. We want the room to look inviting. I have picked flowers, spread sarongs and pillows, and placed a beer-bottle candlestick in the room, which she will share with Nadya in *haus Nadya*.

We cleared out the mud and the mould and organised the schoolroom. What will she be like? everyone wonders. Nadya is afraid that she will be (a) thin, (b) posh, and (c) bossy. Jan is afraid she may not be like

Kate. Mishka is in his own world, indifferent. Tutor or no tutor, he knows it won't make any difference to him.

20 February

Now she's here. One lovely, dry, civilised night in Hagen at the hostel. We washed the mud from our feet and peered oddly in the mirror at our not-often-seen reflections, preparing ourselves to be scrutinised by the newcomer. Voy said he looked stupid, with a 'too-small hat', and why hadn't I told him? I was busy with my own image.

My hair was a thick mass, unkempt and curly from the humidity. I liked the look, and started to vainly play with bits of hair, curling them around my face and admiring the effect. I put on lipstick and eyeliner. And then I spun around and modelled my new look. But Voytek was less impressed than me.

'No, Kot, please no! You want to ride the *curva* bareback ponies in the circus, no?' (He often ends his exclamations with 'No!')

This was not the sort of response I had expected after all my trouble, and I was bitterly disappointed that my artistry was not appreciated. Why is it that this man of mine, who goes on long treks and endures discomforts in order to witness hosts of other people dancing with face-paint on, cannot stand even a little bit of eyeliner and lipstick on his own woman? My little fantasy was washed off in the warm water of the basin and I became me again.

The children, too, tried to look their best to meet Becky. Nadya has taken to wearing several dozen linked safety pins around her neck, an unlikely accompaniment to a string of corals given her by her Polish Jewish grandmother, Babcia. Added to this is a gold drop filigree earring in her pierced ear. Actually, apart from a look of daredevil health, she looks a bit of a mess.

Jan, handsome and stylish, found matching socks and clean trousers. Jan will always be elegant, under any circumstance. With Nadya I couldn't possibly say. Mishka had the blue and yellow tracksuit which has been his preferred garment for the last two years, and I know for certain that he won't want any other until he grows out of it.

So. Becky. We expected her to be short, hairy and with glasses; she was tall and thin, blonde and blue-eyed, with no glasses and a gentle, open manner. We all liked her on the spot, and were relieved. We drove her straight down to Rulna, arriving at our blacked-out hut. Nobody was waiting for us.

Her welcome did not go as planned. On his way into the darkness of the hut, Voy's huge boot crunched on one of the new kittens who had appeared to greet us, squashing it. Numndi picked up the corpse by the tail and flung it a couple of metres across the room where it lay in the full glare of the Coleman light, attracting Becky's fascinated gaze. I threw it further but it didn't help. The damage was done.

Voy started to prepare the evening meal on the kerosene camp stove, cooking with his wonderful panache as if he had not noticed the murderous act of his giant's boot, killing not only the kitten but Becky's entrance to Rulna. He served up the fried chicken and rice, gallantly offering the first serve to Becky.

'Oh,' said Becky, 'I'm a vegetarian. Sorry!'

Now, three days later, she still won't eat. She feels repulsed by the kitten incident, I can tell. She notices the pungent smells and people's disconcerting habit of staring unabashed at close range. She is generally put off.

And of course there is the mud and the rain and the fleas. But tonight Jan made a vegetarian curry and Nadya worked at her French and we all went to eat some of Numndi's *marita mu-mu* and I think I can see signs of settling in. The children of course warned her, graphically, about how your shit and piss goes bright red after eating *marita*, the vermillion, oily fruit of the pandanus. They don't want her to have any more health shocks. They like her being here.

Voy finally left for the Jimmi. He set off early this morning with Ruminj and Kuk, who was carrying a gun, and they disappeared into the forbidding clouds at the bottom of our valley.

24 February

Voy has been gone four and a half days now and I miss him. I've been sick practically since he left, with huge, blistering tonsils and fever on and off. Finally I succumbed to the irresistible temptation of our last small bottle of antibiotics. I was going to try to fight this with my antibodies and save the tablets in case one of the children caught it. But as I can't speak, sleep or swallow and it has been four days, I've decided that my antibodies have gone down the Jimmi with Voy.

Nadya is being difficult and I can hardly get any voice together to reason with her. She's started now on a slavish Pella imitation course, wearing the same clothes (or lack thereof), same safety pins and the possum fur in her ear, and makes the same noises in the same deep voice. Now she is sleeping with Pella and Meri Meta in her bed, which is also Becky's room and bed.

Our poor little ailing guest is getting the full blast. I feel like exploding and being really angry with Nadya, but I have no voice. And if I did have, then Nadya would have some retort which I couldn't answer for fear of offending either Pella, whom I love, or Meta whom I don't love at all but do not wish to offend. They are always beside her.

I am forcing myself to remember being fourteen, and my enthusiastic attachments to all sorts of people who held me in some inexplicable spell for God knows what reason. And I'm also making myself remember what a shocking flirt I was. At the end one emerges with a personality that is perhaps just a distillation of all those influencing elements. Nadya's emergence must be light years away.

Rafal is not too steady on his legs, and has no teeth as he comes up towards twelve months of age—surely a record. He has funny habits which make us happy. He uses a banana as a telephone handset, adopting a concerned expression on his face and saying 'Hullay!' He's been with me many times in Hagen when I've been at the post office trying to phone Australia, and must have been deeply impressed by this process.

I'm not surprised that he has linked the handset to the banana which has nourished him for the last few months. Here the banana is squeezed at one end by the mother's fingers to soften the pulp, then the tip of the skin is cut off with a machete and the baby sucks the sweet, pulped banana through the slit at the end. Just like a bottle. It would be impossible to do this at home where the bananas are all sprayed with hideous toxins. And anyway, we do all the mashing with a fork and then feed it to the infant from a saucer, with a teaspoon, unaware of the inbuilt baby-feeding equipment which is the simple banana skin.

Jan is being charming to Becky, trying to cure her malaise. He is charming anyway, the perfect host. He really likes her. He tries to make her feel at home, inventing vegetable curries for her, and making cups of tea. Mishka, too, is trying to make her welcome, telling her about the local systems, customs and habits. He takes her to the *moka sing sing* up in the Tipeka lands, and explains to her as much as he has worked out for himself. I don't know whether she will ever really like it here. After the last experience of our visitors falling violently ill, I wonder if perhaps our house, now cosy and familiar to us, might be revolting to someone from London, used to pristine hygiene and normal food. Becky looks frail, refined and vulnerable, not like the robust Kate, who wore her tropical ulcers like jewellery and yelled whenever the need arose.

The men have all gone today, planning yet another *moka* at Pri's place, where they discuss the details. The bigman Wei, the one who was dying, has come from Palge with his chief men and now wants to make the next *moka* with the tribe here. He doesn't look too bad at all. Perhaps the pigs being sacrificed to the *tipokais* when we visited have given him a new lease of life. Perhaps the *tipokais* are his drowned wives, who would prefer to keep him in the land of the living. Now, having in mind the two kina he gave to Voytek, he has come to see me with his cohorts in order to beg a lift to town for his son, Councillor Puruwei, whom he says is 'too tired to walk'. I'm being rushed for favours in Voy's absence.

Rain, rain, rain, rain. Mid-afternoon and it's dark already. There's nowhere to go but one's hut and it's dark in there too, so we have to light the lamps. What shall we eat tonight? In vain I try to dream up a menu that might be a change from rice, *kau kau* and a sprinkling of fried meat, but until my swallowing apparatus is restored I find it hard to sustain any interest in food at all.

28 February

It's hard to keep track of dates and the time of day. Voy is coming back tomorrow, we think. My boys, along with Becky, Agena and Punk, a handsome Kawelka adopted by the Gamegai tribe as a baby, are going to leave at 5.30 a.m. to meet him and at the same time get some *rop kunda*, thick, supple bush cane, to make Becky a bush bed. This is something they have been planning. An expedition is in the air and they are excited. I have told Nadya that she can't go. She is furious with me—Agena is going. But that's exactly why I have doubts about it. Agena is so secretive and she becomes secretive around him, a sure sign that something is going on despite her claims that she has dropped him.

I have packed lunch for them: a tin of ham, what stale bread there is left, a pineapple and plenty of cigarettes and matches. And then we watched them as they disappeared into the smoky, drizzly dawn at the edge of the forest. I sent Nadya to do her work but noticed her disappearing up the track with Pella. I sneaked gratefully into my studio.

Voy emerged out of the drizzle just on dusk, excited to be back, quite thin. But he came alone. Where was his search party? It was already dark and raining heavily.

'Why send a search party in this weather? You must be crazy, Kot. Have you got any idea how it is down in that *curva* bush now?' Our sentimental reunion was forgotten. We were suddenly plunged by his words into emergency mode. I started to get the dry mouth feeling as my body followed my mind into the dull void of panic. Voytek's party had been delayed by the flooding river. They had been forced to cut down a tree and make a one-log bridge. It was a wild scene. The river had become a raging torrent. The kids were down there somewhere, and night was beginning its swift descent.

Voy's lack of confidence in the search party returning had transmitted its signals to my core, and I started to shiver uncontrollably. I could not moisten my dry mouth, a symptom of the panic which was gaining the upper hand. Nadya stood next to me, Meta forgotten, her face pinched and white, her attention focused only on her missing brothers.

'Mum, say they will be all right! Just say it!'

'Nadya, they will be all right! Okay?' But my chattering teeth were trying to prevent the words from coming out straight.

Voytek joined us as we peered fruitlessly into the gloom, praying to all the *tipokais* but mainly to Olek, that the search party would materialise. No police rescue here, no radio, no helicopters; just us, and the rapidly encroaching night.

Kints was dramatic. *'Kit!'* he kept saying, shaking his head in a very unreassuring manner. *Kit* means 'bad', 'no good', 'danger' in local language. The welcome feast went unnoticed as we lined up on our verandah to wait. To wait for what? Numndi, Pella,

Ruminj, Dokta, Kints and us. We all became silent, saving our energy. We were listening to the drumming of the rain and the roaring of the river and for the time being we were in their power.

And then, like a part of the dream that I hoped we were living, they emerged from the ominous blackness, meeting our penetrating gaze, stumbling into the light and warmth of the fire. They were wet, exhausted and starving. We fell on each other; we were crying uncontrollably, but not them.

The children were keen to tell their story. They had crossed the flooded river to come back again, swinging across hand-over-hand on the twenty or so metres of bush rope they had collected for Becky's bed. The brave Punk had tied one end of the rope to a tree and the other end around his waist, hauling it through the river and leaving the others holding the slack from the far bank in case he didn't make it. He had tied the *rop kunda* to a tree opposite and returned, swinging himself across the wicked torrent on the stretched rope. Then he had gone back again, after further securing the rope, carrying the boys one by one on his back as the angry river roared below, licking around their feet.

Punk was a hero, the boys said simply. He had saved all their lives. Becky, dexterous and nimble from being the best at high school gymnastics, had hauled herself over, and last of all, bringing up the rear, came Agena.

Once again, they had returned. We were all together, safe and sound. In the lamplight I saw the satisfaction on Numndi's face and Kints' look of relief and delight, which reflected the contentment in my own heart.

5 March

Rain, rain, rain all day. During a break in the downpour the boys and I took Rafal, who is sick, down to the mission. On the way back in the dark and the mud I fell down a steep bank and Rafal and I both got covered in mud. I just felt like crying. We both looked so pathetic. Jan and Mishka rushed backwards and forwards with rescuing bits of plastic and we struggled home.

The rain got heavier and as we sat in the warm *haus kuk*, staring at the fire and listening to the story of Pri's new wife from Punk, we suddenly heard the roar of water. Once again, the river had flooded, carrying with it boulders and bridges and its old banks. It is midnight now and the rain still pounds the little roof but it feels safe, lying here in bed in the dry house, reading and writing by lamplight.

8 March

Dark days, rain and mist, the river muddy and swift. Becky is still sick and has to go to the mission to recuperate between clean sheets and to be able to go to the toilet, not wade down the muddy track to our 'hole type'. She is fragile. I hope she will last the distance. Physically, Nadya is more suitable, healthy and robust, carrying her head *bilum* and walking with her splayed feet, making Melpa-type noises and grunts and generally adoring this basic life as she becomes totally involved in the gossip and daily routines of the people.

19 March—Rafal's first birthday

The boys spent the day decorating the little house with candles, putting a clean cloth on the table. Once again they made a train cake with a candle for its funnel and carriages with coloured icing. Rafal's old teddy bear and his new one, sent by Babcia, sat solemnly beside it. Everyone came in to see it. Once again they were impressed, seeing the train lit up in the dark evening and the display of food. Jan had roasted two ducks in his bush oven. Nadya had made biscuits. Mishka had baked bread. Rafal, dressed in his white nightie, had photos taken beside his cake. It was a success.

26 March

Big problems are rumbling in the background, like approaching thunder. A recent visit from Ongka, a Kawelka man made famous by his role in *Ongka's Big*

Moka, a film by anthropologist Andrew Strathern, has succeeded in stirring up a large number of people against us. They are trying to 'court' us and our immediate close family here, Kints and his sons.

The charge is that we have not distributed the bounty associated with our presence, for instance lifts to town, around the other clans. It seems Andrew had done things differently with Ongka. He had been much more fair, they said. He had donated one car, one hundred pigs and two guns. That's what they told us. Either Andrew was very rich and generous or, more likely, Ongka is simply boasting. Either way, the precedent is fuelling a lot of resentment against us. Now the Gamegai are demanding similar gratitude payments from us. In addition, they feel that Kints and company profit from our being here and they do not. A solemn charge has been handed to Voytek, written on a piece of grubby paper.

Voytek, brandishing the summons, has raged off down the track, and is no doubt now heavily involved in angry discussions with Panna the policeman, the magistrate and various other village office bearers, who, according to Numndi, are the instigators of this treacherous plot. The children are outraged. I am doing my usual job of pacifying all parties, Voytek and the adversaries.

Suddenly I think longingly about Australian soil. What are we doing here? Anyway, the green is almost too green for me now, and there is no rest from the insistent wet. The skies are laden with lethargic moisture which seems to bring bad health with it. Jan has had pneumonia,

Mishka tonsillitis, Rafal an ear infection, and Becky has had her nameless malaise for nearly three weeks, vomiting occasionally but generally just suffering from simple apathy which we dare not write off as heat exhaustion.

I have become like a full-time nurse. We have to take Becky to the doctor in Hagen again, and now there is this court case to deal with. It seems incredible to me that there could be such a wave of ill-feeling towards us from people who have been visiting, laughing, playing with the children, eating my bloody flour, pinching the kerosene and bludging cigarettes. At least that's how I have suddenly started to see it. I feel hurt and disillusioned.

It has suddenly occurred to me how vulnerable we are down here in the bush, totally dependent on the goodwill of a handful of people whose language we don't fully understand and whose ways we will never really fathom, despite having an anthropologist as our leader. I see now that our feelings of security are unjustified, that the tide can turn against us in the most sinister way.

30 March

The past few days have been hectic. Father Josef took our car to Hagen and was unable to get back for five days because of a massive landslide. We've been living on ducks from the mission—elderly, chewy birds whose value as poultry must have reached its use-by date some time ago. We also have flour and pawpaw. I never thought I could be sick of pawpaws, especially the sweet, red-fleshed ones you get here. But now I can hardly stand the sight of them as they sit getting soft in a pile on our verandah with little holes pecked into them by creatures unknown.

On Friday the big court case against us came up, and swarms of people surrounded our house. I was still angry and refused to give breakfast to all those who, it was rumoured, were against us. And of course I had to accept Numndi's advice on this.

Once again, Numndi was in control. He was at his most powerful, manipulating all forces according to his wish. But one by one, almost everyone came and secretly told us that they, at any rate, had 'no truck' with the courting party. Then I had quite a few to feed. I made the damper pancakes, *plour*, quite cheerfully, feeling loved once again.

We were told, by Numndi of course, that Panna the policeman and his clansmen developed this plot. Now they have been exposed, says Numndi with a satisfied gleam in his eyes. Once again Numndi has triumphed. I bet he will want to take *them* to court now.

After this day of high emotion, Voy decided to make a beautiful dinner, with a bedsheet spread on our table as a cloth, an elegant soup, sautéed duck and even a salad. He is a genius for making feasts. I was convinced there was no food, but with his usual ingenuity he collected some spring onion and local greens, *kumu,* chillies and sweet potatoes, and made a soup worthy of the best restaurant. We sat there, with the lamp, having our high-class dinner and revelling in the elegance of the whole event.

And then, out of the darkness, as we started into our second course, it happened. Our dog, Winimp, and Numndi's dog, Menzeli, set off after an innocent passer-by. Yells of pain came ringing through the steamy night, as the dogs' teeth sank into the flesh of their prey. Numndi charged after them, shrieking, and came back to enliven our dinner party by announcing that Gabriel Kei, the passer-by, armed as are all the men here with an axe, had retaliated by cutting Menzeli almost in half.

Back rushed Numndi to fight Gabriel. We had a few more mouthfuls. Numndi came in limping, furiously clutching a handful of his beard and nursing a cut finger, saying that Gabriel and his wife had attacked him and that he was going to sue them. And then, just as we had given our moderate condolences and dressed his wounds, they presented us with the bloody figure of Menzeli, who was—amazingly—alive. Numndi estimated, between sobs of grief, that Menzeli's death if it occurred would be quite expensive for the unfortunate victim of the dog attack.

Menzeli, after unnervingly running round in small circles following his tail for a few hours in front of our dinner party, did die. A gruesome floorshow. He was buried two days later with pomp, dressed, Voytek discovered when he went to the burial, in one of Voy's button-up shirts.

There was nothing he could say, no protest he could make, as he observed the respect and attention given to the dead dog in his best shirt and remembered the way it had been treated while alive. It had been only recently that we'd had to endure Numndi's satisfied account of his castration operation on Menzeli, with a razor blade, to stop the dog straying from home.

A pig was duly presented by Gabriel Kei as initial compensation for the loss of Menzeli and, tied by its hoof, was locked into our abandoned chicken yard. Further recompense would follow after the court case, Numndi assured us. Absurd as this seems, we have begun to have complete trust in all of the wise Numndi's calculations. He has not yet been proven wrong.

1 April—April Fool's Day

Yesterday we went 'caving'. It was a happy walk, giving us no premonition of the disaster awaiting us at Rulna. With some trepidation I left Rafal for the day with Pella, giving her a bottle and rosehip cordial and instructing her about dilution procedures. I had never left him before. We wanted to find cave paintings like the one in the cave in Kukuramp, which has a circle of stick figures dancing. Like Matisse, I thought immediately. Equipped with a powerful torch, boots and bananas, we set off. I had a lovely morning, chatting while we walked along in single file.

Voytek was telling me all his explorer's stories and I made him tell the most scary ones to the children in the vain hope it would convince them to stick together and not race each other on these steep paths. We swam in the cold, high river, scrabbled around in the bush and found a good cave, black and abandoned. But we couldn't find any Matisse-type markings in it of course.

We came home happily, Jan racing ahead as usual. But then we saw him coming back across the one-log bridge, very slowly, carrying Rafal, his face bent over the baby. Behind him were Numndi and Pella, wailing. Something was very wrong, and my knees were shaking so much I became unsteady as I walked towards Jan.

Rafal's skin was slack and his eyes were sunken. He was seriously ill. They said he had *bikpela pek pek wara*—acute diarrhoea. '*Rapus em dai*,' I was told: 'Rafal is dying'.

He was dehydrated, I worked out quickly. Once again, *Where There Is No Doctor* had prepared me in advance. With hands that were trying not to tremble I took my baby and walked across the bridge on legs that were trying not to shake.

The diarrhoea was pouring from him. It smelled of rosehip. The syrup had obviously not been diluted. I had not made my instruction clear enough. We carried him all the way past our house and down to the mission *haus sik*, the whole group surrounding me with their eyes on the little patient. Kewa's assistants gathered in a frightened huddle and asked us respectfully how we thought we should treat him. Kewa was off duty.

The ball was back in our court. We took him home, walking up the steep grade quickly and silently. My feelings had shut down, leaving room only for the emergency which engulfed us. No room for emotions, only actions, quick but steady, calm, alert, and no mistakes. Dokta Miki looked up *Where There Is No Doctor* and read out the instructions for a rehydration drink, which Voytek made up. I knew it by heart, but wanted to check to make sure. Rafal vomited it straight up. Don't worry. Don't panic. Start again. Never rush in an emergency. Dad taught me that. Slowly, more slowly this time, drop by drop, I fed him. The children and Voy made a chain of boiling the water, cooling it, mixing the sugar, salt and tea, measuring it into the bottles, just as it had said in the book.

Rafal eventually started to keep it down: a little at a time, no more than a few drops, then a short rest, then a little more. We held our breath and stopped talking, concentrating on the moment, coaxing the dwindling life back into the depleted little body of our boy.

To us it seemed that time had stopped and was waiting for our small emergency team to do its work, but in fact it was well into the night when slowly, sip by sip, Rafal started to rehydrate. We watched his eyes become normal and his legs and arms become less floppy. By midnight he was his usual robust, pesty self, standing against the window ledge, hanging on, talking his talk, not letting us sleep.

His recovery pushed up against our exhaustion. We didn't mind. I just thanked God, or rather Olek, because we knew that it was he who had guided our hands and steadied our minds. As our *tipokai*, he was looking after us. Pella had just sat in the background, staring at us huddled round her little white baby, with poor Numndi beside her, for once all his cockiness gone. They only returned to their house when they knew he was going to live.

5 April

The week has flown by, one event piling upon another, but we have all been sublimely content since Rafal's deliverance from death. Smaller things have ceased to matter. Voy has been so affectionate and sweet, it seems to me that we could live anywhere and be deliriously happy.

Life here is so adverse in every way one could imagine. Our things get stolen from right under our noses: boots, clothes, bags, money, cigarettes. The dirt and mess which accumulates around our heavily occupied dwelling could easily submerge us in hopeless gloom. The washing never really gets dry, the mattresses are mildewed, we all get sick every few weeks. But if we're alive and happy with each other, none of it matters.

7 April

The big *moka* ended today and we all walked up the steep road and saw the last giving of the pigs, the frenetic crescendo when warriors and pigs come screaming down the *moka* ground, waving and shouting. It's an incredible display of warlike excitement in the intense heat and dust—seemingly wild and crazy but actually strictly ritualised.

The *olga* at the end included one startled-looking albino *kapul* perched on a stick and a special small white pig, heavily made up with red eye rings. Puruwei Kuri, the politician, raved, ranted and sweated under his paint. He has a big belly, unlike the trim Rulna men.

Headdressed, painted men walked round inside the circle of onlookers, shouting their messages and jockeying for space or attention. Numndi, for the occasion, had painted white spots over his whole face and body, giving him a leopard-like appearance, a bit of a departure for a Hagener, but then, as Voytek pointed out to me, they are a very innovative lot. Anyway, we could at least recognise Numndi by his spots.

On the way back down, Mishka started to walk in slow motion, dragging his feet, staggering and having to stop. Impatient to get home after the dusty and noisy day, I kept telling him to 'Hurry up, will you!' But he just got slower, and we had to stop for more rests. Then I felt his skin and noticed the exaggerated blue of his eyes. There was something wrong with Dokta Miki.

12 April

We had to leave for Hagen. Mishka was sick. High temperatures for three days meant we needed help. *Where There Is No Doctor* was not working for us.

The bridge over the Winimp was down and on our last trip we had left the car on the other side of the river. Ironically, the broken bridge reminded me of the day not long ago that the visiting government bulldozer crashed through the bridge and the driver ended up in the water with a huge gash in his head. He was carried to our house, where his bearers called out for Dokta Miki. Mishka produced his box and, without flinching, he brought the edges of the wound together and dressed and bandaged it.

Now Numndi carried Dokta Miki across the one-log bridge to the car, where we discovered that the tyres had been let down. We were nervous, and a bit tired. Mishka sat, hunched and feverish, while Voytek walked down to the mission to borrow a hand pump. It all took so long. The pump didn't seem to be working, but finally the tyres responded, sluggishly.

Mishka was burning with fever. Hardly a word was said on the way. We just endured the bumps and the hazardous road in silence, saving what energy we had left until we reached the top of the mountain and crossed the big wide river at Kotna. Then the road levelled out for the last run to the hospital.

The hospital sent us to Minj, where there was a mission clinic with a pathology laboratory. Blood was taken and we've spent five days in Hagen waiting for results—luxury with a good excuse.

Mishka, it turns out, has glandular fever. We have been told there is no cure, he just has to take it easy. What a joke! Mishka always takes it easy. But now it's official: no more schoolwork. What a relief!

17 April

Easter Saturday. And now we're home. It's hard, coming back after a few days away. Some of our stuff was stolen as it was being carried to the house. It was all the luxury items we had bought for Mishka's sickly digestive system. He has been reading in *My Family and Other Animals* that Gerald Durrell fed his sick apes on a special food called Complan. Searching through the pharmacy, I noticed Complan among the food supplements and bought it for Mishka, in an effort to cheer him up, knowing it would appeal to his particular sense of humour. But the Complan was stolen before it even got to the house. It put us on guard immediately. I don't want to have to be on the watch. I have a sick Dokta Miki and they should realise that. We arranged him in bed, by his little window, where he was going to have to stay for six weeks.

Voytek set about finding the thief, together with Numndi, who was full of ideas about who the culprit could be. I just hoped and prayed that, should the missing items be recovered, Numndi would not feel obliged to take the offender to court over the theft of two tins of Complan, two avocados and one box of barley sugar.

At least twelve people were hanging around waiting to sell us things or to be paid. There is one persistent man with four huge pig troughs—hollowed-out tree trunks—which he would like to sell us. Maria had made a *bilum*, Ko had made two hats, Ping a *bilum*, Kongga two *bilums*. These cost four times as much as those in the Hagen market. I like them much better, though, because down here they're made with bush materials and in Hagen they're more likely to be trade-store wool. But having found out at Hagen that our bank balance is much worse than we imagined, it seems that our financial commitments are crowding out of control. Why does everybody want to sell *bilums* and hats to us anyway? And how am I expected to buy all this Rulna craft?

We feel overcome and the place seems more difficult than ever before, the people hanging heavy, waiting for things with infinite patience, patience which we don't have. Voy feels desperate again. His informants are bored. He gives them coffee and cigarettes to wake them up and they drink it and go. Becky is cheerful but shares our irritation, unlike the children, who continue to relate normally to everyone.

Thinking about easing ourselves gradually out of the place, we have made a very unpopular decision. The children are going to board at the Home School in Cairns for a few weeks, and we shall make a concentrated effort to finish off here and get out before we lose control. Anyway, that is not for a few months. It just seems to be a partial compromise with reality.

6 May

Today is the fourth anniversary of Olek's death. I pray to him that he will make Mishka better, as he helped with Rafal; that he will stop his fevers and make him strong again. 'Look, Olek,' I say. 'Look at him, your boy, how strong he was, and how he just shivers and shakes and lies in his bed. You're his father—do something!' And I imagine him, gently and persuasively influencing the other ancestors on behalf of his beloved son.

The wet season still hangs around like an unwelcome guest who refuses to go home. It disturbs most of our plans but life goes on, mud and all. The children have finished their school term and Becky leaves after an exciting night of *tanim het* at our house, when a few young men come to court her with plumes on their heads. We record all the songs and it continues far into the night, head feathers being passed from suitor to suitor as they place themselves in turn next to her. But Becky does not promise herself to anyone at dawn.

She says she is coming back again. She wants to bring her friend Nicky, so that she will have someone to share the experience with.

9 May

Mishka is no better. Numndi keeps looking at him gravely, saying '*Em bai dai*' (he will die). My medical beliefs are still firmly rooted in the Western tradition which predicts his recovery. Nonetheless, Numndi's intermittent announcements are unnerving. Today we succumbed to his suggestion, heartily endorsed by Ruminj, Dokta, Agena and Pugga, of *mu-mu*ing two ducks outside Mishka's window as an offering to a singular *tipokai* this time, beseeching his intercession on Mishka's behalf. We bought the ducks, the ceremony was performed, and the ducks were consumed hungrily.

11 May

Well, *tipokai* Olek must have done it again, because, would you believe it, Mishka left his bed today and walked! Fever gone, he is devouring a plate of pancakes with all his old greed. Numndi and Ruminj are congratulating themselves, smugly content in the knowledge of our extra indebtedness to them. Four weeks have just about passed, I count, and that's how long the doctor predicted his illness would last, but Mishka definitely attributes his cure to the *tipokais*. And so do the others. And I know that it was *tipokai* Olek.

I have been trying to have serious discussions with Nadya, who now says she may marry Agena and stay here. Although she is only fourteen, to the Gamegai and to her own sense of being a Gamegai, she is a fully grown woman, physically strong and well developed. In fact, because of her strength and willingness to work and carry loads she is prized and coveted by the Gamegai. Numndi and Pella are all for this plan. They even want to discuss pigs. Voy talks to her, I try to talk to her, reason with her, but she listens only to Gamegai. My advice is irrelevant to her. She sees me as being part of another world, a world she has left behind. I seem to have lost my ability to communicate with her. We have to think about sending her back to Australia before this world becomes her only reality.

Rafal walks properly now and keeps saying 'Hullay', clutching not only bananas to his ear but improvising with any old cord or string. Now that Mishka is better, he and Jan have set out on the long trek to Palge with a group of gold prospectors, an efficient-looking team of coastal men who were staying here in a tent for three weeks. It was with some trepidation that we let Mishka go. He is still very thin. But they have promised to carry him if his strength fails on the long climb. We have trusted them, but perhaps we shouldn't have. So tomorrow we too are setting off for Palge.

18 May

Now we're back. We came—me, Nadya, Mishka and Rafal—with two men, Anis and 'Boy' who came from his village to guide us. Boy's real name sounds like Wing Bean, but in his village they all call him Boy, so we do too. Voytek and Jan stayed on at Kenunga, a village on the furthest edge of the Palge tribal lands.

We left yesterday morning and planned to go as far as Councillor Numndi's Palge house. It was supposedly a three and a half hour walk. It took us much longer, a real struggle, heaving ourselves up that huge, never-ending mountain, boulder after boulder. I was puffing and panting, willing my legs to make the next effort. Nadya shot up with heavy Rafal on her back, stopping only to wait for me and Mishka. She has become strong and nimble, never flagging, never slipping or overbalancing, a very different Nadya from the one who first came here.

It was a chance to have a chat. She seemed to listen. I had wanted her to come with me because I had been conscious of her flirting with Punk, now regarded widely as a hero for carrying Jan and Mishka across the river. It is not that I want to protect Agena's interests; quite the opposite. But Punk has a wife, a real *meri bilong wok* (a hardworking woman). She looks a bit old and battered beside the beautiful young Punk, but so what? Everyone gets old and battered in the end, but it doesn't help to have your man making eyes at some fresh young creature with no sense of responsibility because she's not going to stay here anyway. I reason with Nadya; she listens and agrees, at least partially. She's fourteen, flirtatious, and is enjoying her enormous popularity.

'But Mama,' she says, 'what if I choose to stay here for good?'

'That,' I say, 'is out of the question. Forget it.'

She is silent, thinking, no doubt, what a mean witch I am and planning how to outwit me. Our 'back to Australia' plan was broached, and was met with furious resistance. I dropped it for the time being in the interest of the rest of the journey. Anyway, we reached Councillor Numndi's house in the heart of the Palge forests. We stopped for an hour, cutting our pawpaws and sucking them with thirsty relish, eating plenty of red bananas which the people at Palge brought us. Refreshed and full of heart and strength, we decided to move on, despite Councillor Numndi's invitation to sleep in his house, as we had on the way to Palge. We wanted to get back to Rulna.

We dreamed of eating a delicious meal, of sleeping in our beds and washing in our river. My misgivings about going further with Mishka were allayed by his enthusiasm to go on rather than endure another night with eyes smarting from the smoke-filled house where we'd had to constantly pull Rafal away from the fire, loop a pig rope around his leg in case he wandered in the night, try to find scraps of food to feed him and sleep on the hard ground disturbed by the chorus of snores from our hosts.

The first part of the walk back was so beautiful, the mountains high and full of rain mists. Anis and Nadya were singing, harmonising—she in her deep voice, he in a sort of descant. The sound echoed through the mountains. I walked silent, listening, thinking of Nadya as a jungle diva, singing songs of nostalgia and premonition. Was it premonition about her life? Something made me whisper a sudden prayer to Olek to look after his passionate young daughter and stop any forces that might want to destroy her provocative spirit.

What will she *be* in her life? Here you don't have to be anything except who you are. Your competence is immediately recognised for what it is worth in practical terms; like Dokta Miki, already established in his thriving practice at the age of eleven. Back home we have to study and struggle to be able to exploit our talents, our ambition, to earn our living.

There was something in Nadya's echoing voice which wrenched my gut. Hers is the voice of a singer. She is a jungle diva now, free and strong as the river, but what about the future?

A huge storm broke. Suddenly the forest became dark with lightning and thunderclaps, and for the next two hours we had to fight our way through the deep mud which had appeared instantly. The paths turned to rivers and the rivers to torrents; the flimsy bridges were slippery and dangerous.

Nadya carried Rafal, never faltering on the bridges, trying to manoeuvre an umbrella over him while he sat staring at the rain, hanging out of his carry seat. Mishka trudged on bravely, shivering in his sodden clothes. He is still painfully thin. I am terrified that the illness will return after such a physical ordeal.

Mother and child portrait by the author

Numndi, grandson and Rafal

Agena, Nadya's boyfriend

Mishka, Ruminj and Jan building haus Nadya

Rafal's first birthday party

Maria

Dokta Miki's clinic

Rafal with his banana telephone

Christmas decorations as headdress

Mishka with kapul

Nadya's 'arrest'

Numndi

Jan admiring the dancing women

Kathy with nappy on her head

Kints with Rafal and Kathy

Jan and Mishka crossing river on the log bridge

1994

Nadya the singer

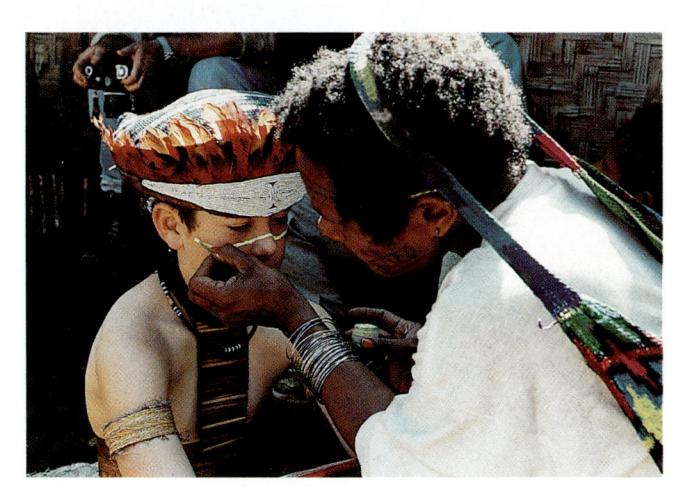

Rafal being decorated by Pella

Highland landscape painted by the author

At last, as night began to close in, we reached the lowest points of Rulna. Anis and Nadya were singing all the way to keep our spirits up. The final steps were painful; my legs had almost stopped obeying my will and were going all over the place. But coming home to the lamps lit by Numndi and the women fussing over Rafal, drying him and feeding him, made me feel it had been worth it. I just sat, speechless, and watched Mishka make the dinner—fried poppadums, after all our food fantasies. And then we just flopped as we were, wet and mud-streaked, and slept.

19 May

A beautiful day, bright and shining, optimistic. I had a wash in the river, letting the water beat on my back, and then I sat for a couple of unusually quiet hours writing my diary.

Afterwards I listened to the gossip. A huge mother pig had died, a pig which was due to be given in brideprice to buy Pugga a woman. They are nervous about this, saying it is a portent, that one of the *tipokais* is angry, that he was hungry and wanted the pig for himself, and that now a man or woman will die too. They must quickly kill an equally big pig and appease the *tipokai*'s hunger and wrath.

And now who should appear out of the blue distance but Jan and a friend. Voy had not turned up when he said he would, so Jan had not waited any longer. Voy must have found plenty to do there.

And then, all things multiplying in the way that they do here, a peaceful morning turned rapidly into a hectic afternoon. Kumu Toga, the Minister for Lands, appeared importantly with his cohorts and loquaciously entertained the company for several hours while consuming our precious and dwindling supplies of food. Being here and being white, we are expected to give hospitality to all visiting bigmen, of whom there are plenty in these parts. Also the whole Palge line has appeared, having hosted us for three days, to receive payment in the form of food and sleeping space. We have four extra people for the night and twelve extra for each meal. Voytek hasn't come. Where is he?

Kuma Toga delivered a loud speech in his own language, and Numndi translated for me, seriously. Kuma Toga, said Numndi, had a proposition to put before us which we should definitely consider.

If he could borrow our Nadya for two weeks, to accompany him to Hagen, he would show her around the high society there and provide the whole of the Gamegai tribe, including our family, with rice, tinned fish and chickens for three months—an exchange so favourable to the Gamegai that everyone was pushing for the deal, which was seen as one we could scarcely refuse. Jan and Mishka, solemn and thoughtful in the face of such a dilemma, voted against, as did Kints. I held my tongue for the moment, interested to see Nadya's reaction.

Nadya's love for the Gamegai, and a sudden vision

of herself as the legendary self-sacrificing heroine of the mountains, had already partly informed her decision, despite the unattractive presence of the ageing politician in his tea-cosy hat, offering a definitely dubious package. 'I'll go,' she announced, her face full of nobility, her bearing as proud as Joan of Arc before battle. Like a queen leaving on a jumbo jet, she scaled the steps up to the back of Kumu Toga's truck.

'No, sorry, I've changed my mind. I won't go.' She made the announcement in pidgin, looking defiantly around her, her eyes blazing. And down she came.

Everybody agreed that she had made the right decision, that Kumu Toga, who had now driven off, was a 'humbug.' They all agreed with her diagnosis of Kumu Toga as a stupid old man, notwithstanding his lofty politician's status. After all, they reasoned, was Nadya not *their redskin*?

20 May

A dark and misty day. I washed the nappies which didn't dry, not even on the rocks. I tried to wash my hair, too, but the Sunlight soap wouldn't lather. My hair feels like cassowary feathers. We cooked all day, preparing for Voytek's return. I was sure he would come tonight, hungry and tired after several days without food or sleep. Mishka made bread, Jan made pizza, Nadya made biscuits and cakes, and I recooked the portion of pork we'd been given after the sacrifice to *tipokai* to ward off the lightning demon. Kumu

Toga had ceremonially presented me with three beers. I put them in the kerosene fridge, which is amazingly effective in this wilderness. We waited.

The evening grew darker and darker and we knew they wouldn't be able to find their way in the bush without a light. That meant they wouldn't come. We looked at the feast and felt a bit flat. Ruminj went with a Coleman light to look for them. Then, independently of Ruminj, they suddenly walked in. Ruminj turned up later. It seems that the opportunity to play cards, illuminated by the Coleman light, had been too much for him, and that's what he had been doing. The reunion feast was under way.

21 May

Now it is morning and big news has broken on the first streaks of dawn making its way over the mountains. We can hear the *bik-mousing,* the yodelling calls from one mountain peak to another. This method of instant communication is as good as a telegram. Better. It sounds thrilling. It's free.

A bigman has died at Tigi—been poisoned, they say—and everyone down here is preparing to go to mourn. Anyone who did not attend the funeral would be suspected of having a role in his death. They will tear their hair, and paint their faces and put mud on their bodies. They will dress the dead bigman in his ceremonial garb and leave him in his house for a few days before burying him. During this time they will sing the ritual mourning songs.

We will go too. I can't imagine anybody would suspect us if we didn't, but you can never be too sure around here. I shall not tear my hair though, and Voy has no hair to tear anyway. As car owners, we are under moderate to strong pressure to attend. The children are excited again at the prospect of another walk through the mountains. Our socks are hardly dry and our boots stiff with mud, but the excitement of the walk is still in our veins.

But now, because the bigman has died, the peace negotiations with the neighbouring enemy tribe, the Mabege, must be hastened. It has to happen before the funeral, because after the funeral there will be an official period of mourning commensurate with the 'bigness' of the dead man. And this dead man was very important.

22 May

Once again, the calls went out over the hills, summoning the distant Mabege to celebrate the peace offering party. We heard them yodelling and calling for hours, *bik-mousing* across the mountains. Ruminj and Kints asked Voytek to take them in his car up to the 'club' in Rung, where a tin shed for drinking beer is guarded by a watchman with a bow and arrow. There they were to collect the thirty cartons of beer to be given to the Mabege. Rung is an hour's drive away, but Kints' request is considered to be a command.

So Voy went. The peace party will go all night, and tomorrow all the Rulna Gamegai, except for the old people, will proceed over the mountains to the funeral at Tigi.

23 May

When night fell we went to observe the ritual giving of the beer to the Mabege. Twenty cartons were arranged like an altar. Ten remained inside the house of the court magistrate, Pri. The reason for this, we discovered, was that the givers only partook of their own beer when the drinking started, hence the ten cartons. The receivers, the Mabege, drank the other twenty. On one side of the altar sat the Gamegai and on the other, their oiled bodies glistening in the light of the moon, were the Mabege.

First, the Gamegai made lengthy speeches about the cause and the course of the tribal wars, and then the Mabege replied, some becoming excited and angry at the memory of past outrages. Then Kints, the old man, got the idea that Mishka should talk. There was a bit of an argument about this. Some agreed, some were against. But Kints insisted. Mishka climbed onto an upturned 44-gallon drum.

I felt quite a big lump in my throat as I watched my little eleven-year-old standing up bravely in front of all the half-naked warriors and making his small speech, his white hair soft in the moonlight, his voice high, his well-known logic never faltering. He spoke slowly in pidgin to the congregated tribes, recalling the times when we had first come, when the Mabege had been regarded as enemies and the Gamegai had been afraid to walk in their territory. 'That was bad,' he said, 'and has to be fixed up. You can't have people going around in fear. Two tribes in alliance are stronger than two tribes at war. So now with this peacemaking party everybody will live and be able to walk freely in each other's territory. So this must be a good thing.'

Everyone clapped. Kints, like me, had tears in his eyes. We took the orator home to bed, anticipating our early departure for Tigi. The speeches must have stopped and the drinking started. All night and through to dawn I could hear the droning singing voices of the men filtering into my sleep, the refrains and crescendos in a minor key which had now become one of the familiar sound effects of our strange life in these mountains.

26 May

Nadya, Jan and Mishka opted for walking, and they left early with several Gamegai. Kints, always concerned about the children, offered to make the day last longer by using his rare powers of slowing down the passage of the sun. It must be an indication of how long I have been here that I felt genuinely grateful to him for his promise.

Tigi can be also reached by road, so Voytek and I drove. We took Rafal, Councillor Kongga from Tigi, who was visiting Rulna, and Ruminj. The three-hour trip—up the Hagen road, then turning off the road at Tigi—was quite eventful. We had to negotiate a roadblock where some men insisted we had left their gate open, thus allowing their garden to be ruined by marauding pigs. In vain we argued with them that this was not the case, that we had never been in this area.

Finally Voytek just accelerated and knocked down their flimsy barrier and we drive on at high speed over the rough terrain. Ruminj and Kongga were impressed; I was apprehensive, fearing fierce consequences.

When the track stopped we left the car and in single file walked through the gardens towards the funeral. Kongga and Ruminj ceased their chitchat, started to pull their hair and beards, and set up a sort of wailing cry. Amazed and somewhat embarrassed by the abrupt change in their behaviour, we continued with them, wondering whether perhaps we should be tweaking our own hair.

Then, as we rounded a bend in the track, we spotted the crowd. We were approaching the scene of mourning. We followed the mourners, all gathered around a small circle of intense activity which seemed to involve more weeping and tugging at hair and beard, and caressing of the dead man's bark belt and *bilum*, which hung in a tree.

The family moved around this tugging and weeping activity, wailing loudly and singing in loud, swelling voices the dirges to the dead man. They sang about how he was here and now he isn't, how beautiful was his skin, how he won't be here tomorrow.

'Oh, my brother! How will you help us, when you are gone?'

It was very moving and dramatic except that the whole thing was taking place in the searing, dusty heat and there was little or no shelter, every tree having been already taken up. There was no food either, as the food brought could only be distributed by the bereaved family. The family was to use these offerings to feed the throngs of mourners who had travelled for days across the mountains to pay homage to the dead man. The pile of goods and money grew and grew but we were not offered anything from it, although the sugar cane looked fresh and juicy, and the bananas sweet. It seemed that the visiting mourners had to wait for their sustenance.

We sweltered there for awhile and Rafal was getting filthy and desperate. Someone showed us to a small stream which was more like a bog. We washed him in the bog, and ourselves too, and drank a little of the bog water. I was getting edgy and fractious, demanding that Voy abandon his anthropological duties and get me and Rafal right out of the place.

Then we saw the Gamegai approach in a group, looking slightly unfamiliar as they were tearing their hair and wailing while walking. We scrutinised the group, hoping that our children were not also ripping out their hair somewhere in the middle of the delegation. I would not have put it past Nadya. But they were not there. Insensitively, I interrupted the grievers.

'Where the hell are they?'

'They stopped in another part of Tigi to meet you.' Tug, tug, wail. They kept moving, at a fast pace along the track. I followed them.

'What part? Where? Whose house?' Their eyes were glazed, mesmerised by their chant. I gave up and went back to Voy who was standing waiting for me, mounting impatience in his eyes. Impatience with me? After all, I was the one who had insisted on coming. I should have stayed in Rulna and left him to his manly duties.

Nobody knew or cared where the children were, so I decided to go and look for them. Voy had to take me. I don't think he was sorry to leave this inferno. Eventually we found Nadya and Jan, but no Mishka. Councillor Kongga wanted to take us to his house. He said that Mishka might be there because he was last seen with Kongga's brother Pig. I had never heard of Pig and did not like the sound of him, especially his name. Unconvinced, we had no other leads. We had to try, despite the considerable walk involved in reaching Kongga's house. We waded across two rivers and up hills, and then, as the approaching darkness was making me nervous, we saw him, Malu Malu intact on his shoulder, coming out of the setting sun, towards us. He was earnestly chattering with Pig, his guide. He hadn't been able to keep up with the brisk uphill pace that Nadya and Jan had set, so he had been walking slowly and had taken seven hours to complete the arduous climb.

'Mum,' Jan whispered to me with tears in his eyes, 'Kints' sun magic worked for Mishka!'

So on we went, reunited, to Kongga's house. We prepared our evening meal of rice and tinned meat and distributed it to our hosts. Kongga gave us his house. I attempted sleep with Rafal on a bed made of cardboard beer cartons full of empty bottles—not a soft repose. Voy slept on a cane stretcher made for someone half his size. The children slept on the floor, soundly.

We woke to the noises of morning and the smell of fire. It was cold after warm Rulna, so high. It felt like the mountain tops. And there was planted grass around, which we took advantage of, sitting and lying in it, letting Rafal crawl around. A break from the mud which surrounded all houses at Rulna. This part of Tigi is beautiful.

Cold streams and high trees and the feeling of luxury after our previous stay here with Kate at the *sing sing* ground, where we had drowned in stinking mud and had our boots stolen. At Kongga's place there was always a fire, always water and we wisely brought our cups and plenty of dried milk, which was a saviour at times like this, giving energy to exhausted bodies.

2 June

The mourning finished and we left, first the children, walking, and then us, by car. We got back in the evening after spending several hours in the dusty heat beside the car, waiting for the return of the man who had been guarding the car's contents in his house.

We had promised to transport a pig back for Pella. I didn't want to take it. Voytek insisted. It shrieked and shat in the back of the car. Pella giggled, muffled its mouth, remonstrated with it. Voytek swore and abused Pella for misleading him about the size. It was a big mother pig, not a baby as she had promised.

The trip was slow and bizarre, with the big pig squealing and struggling on our laps. Regretting his generous decision, Voy kept threatening to throw it out, but Pella just giggled her throaty giggle, Voy looked uncertain and the pig stayed. Eventually, we got back to Rulna, but the children had not arrived. Once again, where the hell were they? Search parties were sent up the mountain. Then, just as darkness fell, the weary travellers returned.

But rest was not to come—not yet. The next day we left for the Jimmi Valley. I was sick of being always left at home, waiting; we wanted to see the Jimmi too, even knowing that it is a good two- to three-day walk. It would be me, the three children, Pri, Moka Tipeka and a Gamegai from Tigi called Josef. Tremulously, I left Rafal with Voytek and Numndi along with a list of instructions which I knew wouldn't be followed. We wouldn't be back for five days. A long time to leave Rafal when I'd never left him overnight before. Kints and Numndi were nervous about our going. Kints was entirely against the plan.

'Kot!' he said, his expression dramatic.

I agreed with him, but was too far into the plan to drop it. Kints' warning of *sangumas*, their deadly exploits and their extreme power in the Jimmi territory just left me feeling very shaky about embarking on what seemed to be a ridiculously risk-laden journey for a woman who really needed to survive.

We quit our tiny home, said worried goodbyes and struck off down the valley. We walked and walked and finally arrived, exhausted, at a bush shelter deep in the forest, a raised mat of leaves on sticks under which we tried to sleep for the night. The men were afraid in the bush; they didn't sleep but sat by the fire all night, singing songs and telling stories. They were very happy when we woke up and joined them.

Another long toil through the jungle, trudging and wading, slipping and clambering, and then, like a miracle, the Jimmi River appeared, blue-flowing, wide like the sea and spanned by an amazing swing bridge made of bush string and sticks. It looked precarious. The children immediately started to run over the bridge which swung and bounced with every step. I watched, unable to prevent them.

We felt uplifted, excited, as though we had arrived in a new country. Then Pri and Josef *mu-mu*ed the snake they had captured. Not delicious, it tasted like snake. But it was food. We had a good rest and bathed ourselves in the warm river. The children played while I washed the socks and clothes and dried them on the hot stones. The children sat on the men's shoulders, waist-deep in the fast river, having cock fights.

Just before evening we continued our journey, crossing the swaying bridge, and finally arriving at Tsandiap, the place where the gardens are biblically beautiful and the people are small and pock-marked and speak a different language. There was much talk about where we should sleep, and an ex-*kiap* house was allotted us.

The men made a fire, pulling the wood from the walls of the house for firewood, and we cooked our rations: rice and tinned meat. Unable to face tinned meat anymore, I just ate pawpaw which the local women brought. I knew I wouldn't sleep too deeply, as here in the Jimmi we all had to sleep together, side by side. We had to protect our men, who were genuinely afraid of the *sanguma*.

I put Nadya between me and the boys, and then the three men. One cannot be too cautious, I thought. None of the men left our side and they hid all day in the house. None of us moved too far, resting our aching limbs and drinking coconut milk to recover.

Tsandiap was different to Rulna—lower, more tropical, with coconut trees, exotic like a resort. Everything was still, the sun fierce, the night beautiful. We seemed so close to the stars, which were bright above the silhouettes of the coconut trees. The distant laughter from the village made the men curious. It was women's laughter, inviting, taunting, stirring their imagination. They started discussing the local women and how to buy some wives for themselves. These Jimmi women were known as hard workers, small and pock-marked as they were, compared to our hefty beauties in Rulna. But not one of those men would have had the courage to marry a Jimmi woman. The Jimmi were too linked in their minds to the *sanguma*. They were just enjoying the fantasy.

The next day we left on the long trek back, laden with spears which the boys had bought after a day of bargaining and haggling. Many times they nearly 'de-eyed' me with the ends of the spears as we trudged in single file along the narrow bush track. In the evening we camped by the Jimmi River, but alas, we were not allowed to sleep at all. Our three guides were now really terrified of the Jimmi spirits. They were busy making barriers over the paths to stop spirits coming and they did not want us to sleep but to sit up with them all night guarding the barriers.

'Why,' I asked, 'would a flimsy barrier over a path stop a spirit?'

'Because they always travel on the paths,' they answered.

Then suddenly, out of the black gloom of the forest appeared a Jimmi man with three dogs. Pri and the others were transfixed with fear. The man and his dogs had easily negotiated the barrier. They stood outside the circle of the fire.

'Give him some food!' they whispered to me,

hoarsely. I was irritated by their demand, as we had planned our meagre menu carefully, making no allowances for a man and three dogs. But the urgency in their eyes made me go along with their command. The man ate, fed his dogs and left, crashing through another barrier in the direction of the Jimmi.

'Why did I have to give him our food? We hardly had enough for ourselves.'

'They are *sangumas*!'

'They are not *sangumas*, they're just a man and three dogs on a hunting trip!'

'Look, you don't know, trust us, we know. If you're nice to them and give them food they may not do their magic on us!'

They re-secured their barriers over the paths, but this security measure, having failed once, allowed them no feelings of safety. I knew they would not let us sleep. They sang love songs to Nadya, *tanim het* songs; they told stories; they made us sing too—anything to prevent us from sleeping. The night was endless. Nobody carried a watch.

I wanted to leave at dawn, but the first pink streak across the sky relaxed their vigilance and permitted them to sleep. Now the night spirits could no longer attack them. The spirits had gone to their own sleep. I was close to despair. I thought we would never get away. My whole body had been eaten by fleas, ants and mosquitoes. My knee had been bitten by a spider and sported a huge red swelling. I longed to go home, to rest, to eat, to wash. I was impatient to see Rafal.

The sun was high in the sky before we got the party back on the track again, but eventually after several hours walk, we reached the bridge across the river. We were slowed down by Josef's announcement that he had *pek pek wara* and a fever, and needed to rest at ten-minute intervals. But then, who should be there crossing the log bridge over the Mogilpin River but Voy, Becky and her friend Nicky. A meeting party. I was afraid. Why had they come? My heart was beating rapidly as we approached each other.

'Rafal's okay,' Voy assured me. 'Pella is looking after him.'

I realised I should just be happy to see Voy and the girls, so I was. My heartbeat returned to normal.

Becky had returned to Rulna with Nicky and they had all come to meet us. We had a lot to talk about as the evening settled over the bush. They had brought new rations with them: sardines, chocolate and cheese which we instantly devoured. It was just as well they had food for us, as we had given practically the last of our rations to the *sanguma*.

We snuggled down on the warm stones by the river to sleep. The water gurgled past our heads and our beds, and the next day we walked home, reaching Rulna in the late afternoon. I rushed up the last hill towards Rafal, although my legs had difficulty receiving any instructions. He greeted me somewhat coolly from his comfortable perch on Pella's broad hip. She proudly delivered him to me and he looked perfect. His hair was freshly washed and he had red daubs painted on his face. On his upper arms he had little straw armlets.

'Hullay!' he said, and then he whimpered and somewhat reluctantly stretched out his arms to me.

'I've been to the Jimmi,' I said, 'and one day you'll come too!'

Then the others arrived and his eyes really lit up. His world was restored.

Never did the house look so comfortable and the beds seem so soft. We stuffed ourselves with bread, butter, jam, hot cups of tea, washed our hair and feet in the river, cuddled Rafal. All together again.

But we are not going to be together for long. The big separation which we all dread is coming. The children are going back to Australia, to school in Cairns. Our other world is looming up again and we have to try to ease them back into it. Rafal and I are going with them, leaving Voy with Becky and Nicky, who are going to be his field assistants and help him chart the territory.

25 June

All the talk has been about the children leaving. Agena took Nadya and Jan down the river for a fishing trip. He returned with an injured hand—a rock had fallen on it—so the trip failed to cheer anyone up. Gloom settled over our little place as we prepared for the departure. Jan sat for days making small paintings of his Rulna home. I felt weighed down by my decision, which suddenly seemed to be pointless. Why, after all, should we be separated?

2 July—on the plane

The goodbye party for the children was a disaster. It was too sad. Everybody cried: the children, their friends, their adopted fathers, mothers, grandparents. I sobbed too. Presents were given by a long line of givers, the gifts tied with red flowers: spears, bush jewellery, possum furs, *bilums*, a bow and arrow for Jan and Mishka, two shields.

This morning we all set off, silent and brooding, up the mountain track in the Toyota. We had said, hoping it would be true, that the children could come back for their next school holidays. That lessened the pain, for me as well. Finality would have been intolerable.

17 July

The transition was not easy. We felt immediately homesick for Rulna. There was no excitement about the journey; it was more of a sentence, something that had to be done. And was there any good reason for such a decision? Perhaps not. Moresby, the plane, and Cairns. David Miller, my brother, who is a doctor; his wife, Nean; and Helen and Steve Wiltshire, our cousins—they made it bearable.

Today we went for a sail around the reef on David's yacht. The sea was blue and turquoise at the edge, and the salt foam flew on my face, trying to cure me of my heartache at the parting which was haunting me.

The older children started boarding school, going like animals to the slaughterhouse, despite the fact that this live-in school bore none of the marks of boarding school as I had understood it. The children wore no uniforms and most of the time, no shoes. There were plenty of Aborigines from the gulf country, and a few Papua New Guineans.

And then Rafal, upon first contact with civilisation, pulled an electric jug of boiling water onto his small, naked body. His screams seemed to come from another world. After doing the cold shower thing, all the steps I had learned in *Where There Is No Doctor*, I tried to find David. Dokta Miki was at school. David had gone to buy a kitten.

Eventually he returned with the kitten. Down to the surgery we rushed and he did a few things not advocated in *Where There Is No Doctor*. He gave morphine, covered the body with cortisone cream, and dressed all the burns with special non-stick dressings. Rafal's little body was like a bandaged mummy.

For days we waited and watched—David, with his doctor's face and his glasses, feeling Rafal's feet, telling me to 'wake him up a bit', peering at Rafal's bandaged face, giving him more morphine, measuring the pulse. I constantly scanned his gaze for any fears he secretly harboured about Rafal's survival. 'Why don't you put him in hospital?' I asked David. 'He's safer with us, right here,' he assured me, telling me of the dangers of cross-infection in the hospital. I had to administer watermelon juice in an eye dropper, to give him potassium, a drop a minute for two days and nights, taking turns with David, noting amounts taken on a sheet of paper, waiting for Rafal to pee.

The children were away at their school, unaware of the seriousness of Rafal's condition. We had been together for all those other emergencies and had done well. This didn't feel right, but I had no energy to change things. Rafal needed everything I had. Once again my emotions seemed to be on shut-down in order to deal with the situation. Emotions take too much valuable energy. Olek was guiding my hand, making me a good nurse, keeping me patient, staving off exhaustion and despair.

The first pee came after twenty-four hours. I could read in David's eyes that it was a turning point. Now Rafal would stand a good chance of surviving. I had written to Voy, aware that it wouldn't reach him for two weeks. The first pee was vital but there were other mileposts to pass: the danger of infection, dehydration (once again), and we didn't know about his sight. I kept vigil, sitting with the bandaged, sedated little creature, who seemed to be in another world.

Three days later, David tentatively removed the dressings. Rafal's blue eyes emerged, seeing us. His skin was red and papery, but he was out of danger. He took two steps towards the children, who were home for the weekend, and said, 'Hullay!' He had made an astounding recovery.

I wrote a new letter to Voy, posted it, urgent. Rafal was out of danger. Thanks to David. Thanks to *tipokai* Olek, operating internationally.

But the next sad departure loomed. I had to go back, leaving Nadya and her brothers in the Home School. There was even a mum and a dad figure there, as substitutes, to make the children feel at home. But our children were not fooled. They hated the school. And, from what I could gather, the mum and dad did not fully appreciate them. The children felt alienated, abandoned, angry.

Mishka got sick. He kept throwing up. I took him out of school and left him with David. He said his belly felt like a vacuum. I got onto the Air Niugini flight with eyes swimming and a choking throat, doubting my decision but having to stick to it just because it had been made. How many decisions do we stick to for that flimsy reason? I wondered uselessly.

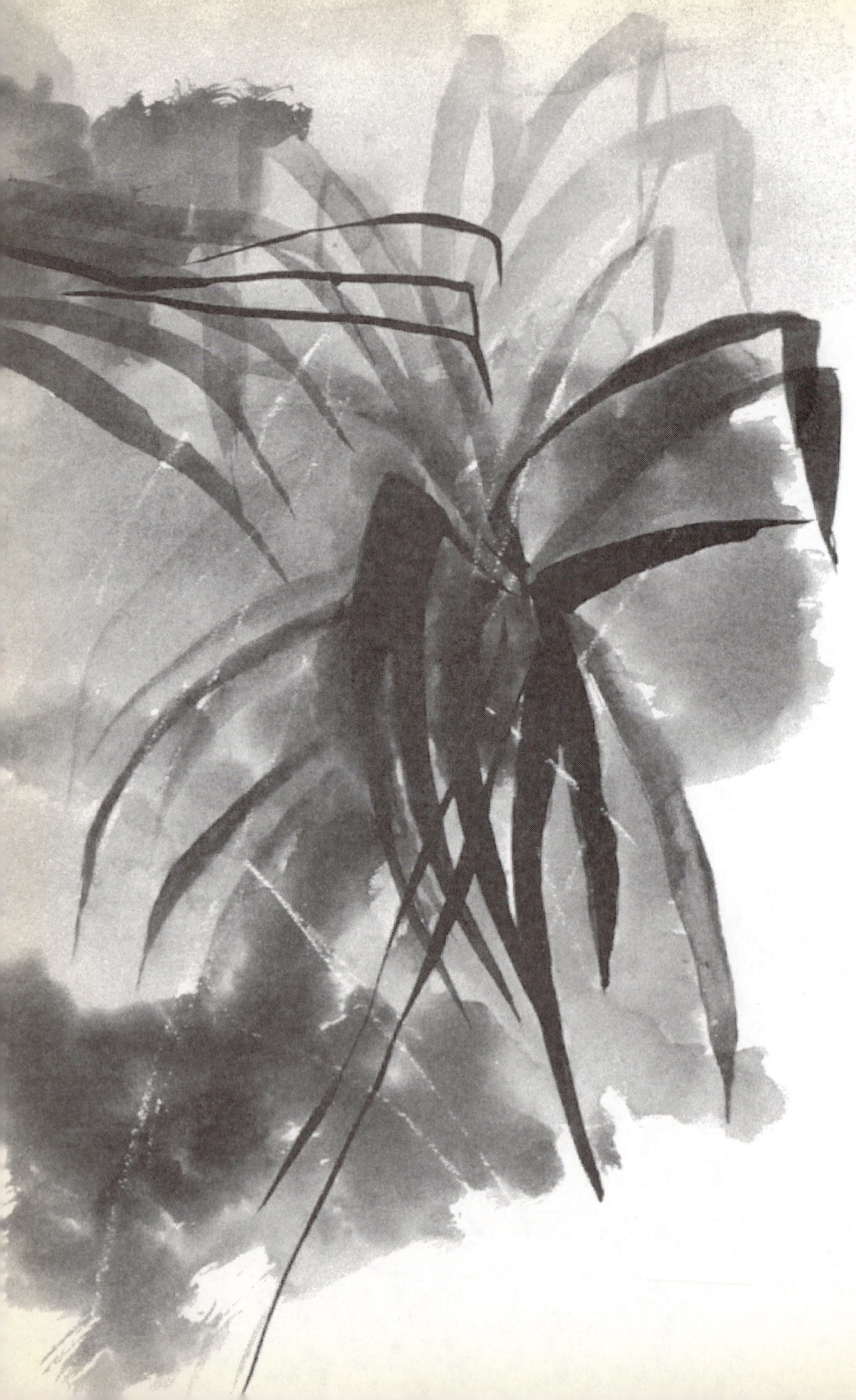

Three Refugees

21 July

Back again, down the bumpy road, down past the cold mists, past the mountain gardens, down into the warm valley. Rulna awaits, lamps lit, Pella excited to see Rafal who, after some initial trepidation, is pleased to be back. Voytek thinks he looks big and very advanced and is touched at the greeting he gives his papa. I am glad to be back, too. Voytek is excited.

Much has happened during my weeks away. A village elder died and there was a great funeral here in Rulna. Three pigs were struck by lightning behind our house. Voy and the girls have done a lot of work charting the territory, counting pigs and wives and making maps of all the adjacent areas. Becky and Nicky look excited, proud of their work. They are different, more hardy and confident, talking pidgin with great panache. They are old hands now, but are about to go back to Australia and then to university in England to begin their studies in—guess what?—anthropology.

23 July—Voytek's Birthday

Now the girls have gone, tearful and tatty, looking far from the neat products we met when they arrived. Nicky had a torn old dress of Nadya's done up with a huge nappy pin, boil scars all over her legs and the remains of a fungus on her face.

A few days in Hagen for me and Voytek. Voytek was suddenly fed up—didn't want to go back to our place, wanted a rest, a bit of luxury, a change. So we cruised for a few days, visiting, phoning the children. Rafal said 'Hullay' in the telephone and Jan started to cry. Then I started to cry too, attracting the stares of the other twenty people in the telephone queue. But I had made a secret resolve: the children were coming back, whatever.

We wondered how to celebrate Voytek's birthday. (Finally, a rest from the train cake!) We bought some whisky from the bishop and arrived to spend the night with Father Jan, a Polish missionary living outside Hagen. He took us over to some friends of his, John and Edith Watts, and they invited us to dinner. So that was the birthday dinner. Candles, three courses, a bottle of wine—a good birthday, and a complete surprise for us.

We were curious about them, and about their very

charming, unpretentious house. John Watts, we discovered over many whiskies, had flown Lancaster bombers for the RAAF during the war. Unable to settle back into Australian suburbia afterwards, he departed for the colony of New Guinea with his handsome young wife Edith, a nurse, and their children. On an ex-serviceman's loan they set up their coffee plantation, Ulya, which is now run by their two sons.

John Watts had been a member of the New Guinea Parliament. We talked into the cool of the night, listening to stories of the early days. We had coffee in bone china cups and brandy in brandy balloons. We were in a very contented mood when we finally went to bed at 3.00 a.m.—all of us, including Father Jan.

The next morning we slept late. We felt on holiday. Our hosts were warm and indulgent. In the morning we had coffee from a silver pot. The large, elegant house was made of bamboo and *kunai* thatch. It had corridors, bathrooms, a dining room, a huge country kitchen. The bathrooms had coloured bottles of perfume and talc.

As we drove out of the plantation in the morning, we saw the rows of well-groomed coffee trees, which looked very different from the tiny coffee gardens at Rulna.

28 July

Back to work. Voy is having long and earnest conversations with the indefatigable Dokta. Dokta has an intellect which in another society would make him a great writer or a professor. Here he is respected, but without the necessary attributes for 'bigmanship'. He is too retiring. He is also cave-chested, lacking the bulging muscles associated with the bigmen. Kints, the super bigman, was certainly both proud-chested and pushy when he was young and at his most spectacular. Now, having exploited his youth and bravado to become one of the most famous men of his day, he is still looked to for guidance and is a true figure of authority.

Numndi and Pella have caught a *kapul* and an eel which they are *mu-mu*ing. They always find something to cook and eat in the dry season. It really is a *gutpela taim* (good time) and there is a feeling of joy in the air as they all make fires outside, cooking and eating small catches from the bush. It crosses my mind uncomfortably that perhaps the *kapul* is Malu Malu, who has once again disappeared, abandoning his pouch and his eternal scufflings in the parmesan tube. I decide not to partake of this feast.

Ruminj alone is despondent and aggressive. He is attempting to stand for the competitive council elections. He is being rivalled by formidable candidates, two of them within the Gamegai tribe, so his election is by no means assured. He asked for six kina to pay his tax, telling me that if it wasn't paid he would go to prison. I gave it to him, discreetly, knowing I should have refused and resolving not to tell Voytek and bring trouble on my head.

1 August

Council elections, big excitement. I made a poster for Ruminj, which he still displays. Numndi campaigned for him. We paid our taxes to the official, Wamp, and his underlings, who sat solemnly down below to conduct the elections. Some said we should vote and others said we couldn't vote, so we didn't, we just watched. Cui won with fifty-two votes; Ruminj was runner-up with thirty-five. Disappointment.

Undaunted, Ruminj congratulated the winner and announced that he would now stand for the position of Village Court Magistrate. Voy and I held a dinner to which came Councillor Kuk, Councillor Numndi, Ruminj, Kewa, Kunjil, his father Mak, Mel and Koipa from Tigi.

The weather is still dry, very dry, and people wander at night with flares and lights, looking for fish and game. They like the dry season.

Rafal has this funny habit of donning a hat, or an armlet, or even holding a stone axe, and immediately adopting the Hagen dance rhythm or chant, 'aher-ah'. Everybody laughs and eggs him on. He likes the dry season too.

I think about the children at the Home School and then we get a pathetic letter from Jan. Unable to bear the Home School any longer, they have all taken off, run away and installed themselves at David's place. They go to school from there. I'll have to get them back. School can wait.

And in the same mail we receive a letter from my brother.

Dear Kathy

Thank you for entrusting me with the care of your kids. It is quite a challenge. I have had them for just a short time now since you returned to Rulna. Believe me, they don't want to be here in Australia, even if it is tropical Cairns. These kids are very homesick for their tribe in the deep woods.

Last night Nadya refused to sleep in the house and set up a sort of camp under the back steps. During the night it rained and she was washed out. She then took off into the bush at the back of the house and got lost. She started to call out in a haunting highland wail. Her brothers got upset and, after a hasty conference in pidgin, the little boys set out into the dark scrub and brought her back.

They all talk pidgin as their first language. They look out for each other and unilaterally refuse to attend the boarding school you sent them to. As their uncle I feel helpless that I am not really giving these little refugees what they need. I also have a feeling that reacclimatisation may take awhile and indeed that they may never recover from the Niugini experience.

With love and anxious to hear from you,
David

We struggle here on a pittance and I cross my fingers that we will have money for the children's holidays. Then I will just extend their holiday indefinitely. We have all but stopped buying supplies, living on *plour* and one meal a day. Voy looks thin, but all the better for it I tell him. He has cut his beard and looks very businesslike, in keeping with his present efficient regime.

6 August

We went to Hagen to stock up, ring the children and rest a little, taking Numndi, Pella and Maria, our closest friends here. With Mikel Kewa the *dokta* they formed a cheerful crowd and we sang and joked all the way to Hagen. We took them to lunch, first buying thongs for Numndi, Pella and Maria, who were not allowed barefoot into the restaurant.

Then we dropped them at the house of their *wantok* Raima, who has a little hut on the side of the runway at the airport. We went to the hostel, where we spread ourselves out and wrote our letters, read the mail, made the phone calls. Worrying news from home. Our tenants have paid no rent and have gone, leaving the house in a great mess. In Cairns, the children are homesick for Rulna.

Coming home again, the little house dark and smelly. All the kittens had returned to the maternal home and were whining, skinny and sick. We had to clean up their messes and throw away rotting food, light the lamps and generally cope again. Suddenly, after the privacy of the hostel, it seemed that there were a lot of people here to greet us and share our food. Ruminj has been working himself up into a state of intense anxiety, thinking we are planning a secret departure and wanting to know now what we would give to him. And why do we take Numndi and not him (for it has been decided that Numndi will come to Australia with us for a holiday when we go)?

8 August

The Jimmi boys wait here with anxious eyes for Voy to go with them to the Jimmi. Voy is heavy hearted, cranky about going away again. He won't speak, won't pack. The dry season has broken early, with storms and more storms. Dust has become thick mud and the skies are dark. It is morning and Voy has to go. He sets off, forlorn and miserable in the rain, looking unconvinced, and goes down towards the distant mountains, now shrouded and invisible with cloud.

Rafal has been shitting all night, and I am clutching him, trying to keep him from the dirt, the mud, the pigs, the mess. But he has his own ideas and very soon, as usual, I give up trying and off he goes with his beloved Pella, her children, and her baby pig. I will go and find him at lunchtime, having prepared a nice clean meal for him of rice and vegetables, and he will be standing there in Pella's house, already fed to the eyeballs on all the things I've forbidden while he's ill: breadfruit, taro, corn. I hope no *marita*—that turns his *pek pek wara* red.

Now he's asleep. I sit here and there's not a soul in sight. Siesta time. It's so peaceful and I think of Voy on his long and lonely march. I hope he won't slip on those one-log bridges. And now I have to prepare myself for a week here alone, painting, walking, reading a little, keeping my ear to the ground for gossip and scandal. I think that after all it will go quite pleasantly, and when Voy comes back I shall bake all day and wash the sheets and scrub the table. If he doesn't turn up it will be an anticlimax, a flat evening. I will do the same the next day, looking down the valley for his figure emerging from the parting mists and the *kunai* grass, exhausted, dirty and sweating, dreaming of home and of me.

11 August

Things are beginning to go wrong. Rafal vomited three times last night and again this morning. The old bogeys—dehydration, fever—haunt me and are worse without Voy. I count the days till he comes back but they're too many. Don't count yet, I tell myself.

Numndi and Moni are beginning a new garden, and they spend all day cutting trees, burning and slashing in order to plant cocoa, taro, bananas, peanuts, tapioca . . . even beans. They have left Pella with me. The day dragged. Rafal was whimpering and unable to walk, lying on the bed, his eyes shadowy and unhappy, his legs inert. Then Pella left for the garden, too, and I felt alone and helpless, unable even to go to the toilet without someone to watch Rafal. I started giving him his rehydration mix: water, sugar and salt. Then this afternoon he struggled up again and his usual sounds reappeared. I took him down to the mission to while away the time.

Henry, a visiting missionary, came in angry, saying, 'Josef has had about enough of you fellows. Your bloody cheque has bounced again. No more cheques.' Sometimes the mission cashes cheques for us, to save us going to the bank in Hagen. I sat quietly, playing the humble, appeasing role. It would be too bad to have maintained good relations with the mission for eighteen months and then let it all blow to pieces over money.

I soothed Henry, saying that we would pay, don't worry, and then I cheekily induced his good humour by promising him a little whisky. So he drove me home and I emptied half of our dwindling supply into a bottle and gave it to him. We were friends again. I will keep the rest for Voy when he comes back. Just one sip for me now to soothe my inflamed nerves.

Numndi and Pella and Moni have come in, blacker than usual after their day's work, and I am grateful for their company. They stay the night here with me while Voy is away. Numndi sagely says that whereas everyone around is scared of Voytek, no-one is scared of me, and therefore they would have no compunction in stealing everything they could lay their hands on while Voytek is absent.

12 August

It rained softly all night. Rafal was wakeful, still very thirsty, and I lay there trying to ignore the rat scuttling overhead, knocking bits of roof rubbish or its droppings (I didn't like to think too specifically) onto the bed. I thought, lying awake, how close Voy and I had become here, how dependent on each other, how I missed his body next to mine, how without him it was hard to conquer the feeling of flatness. With the children here I survived when he was away. We still had a busy routine; Rafal was happy. Now I feel very alone and it makes me more conscious of things that don't normally get to me: the cat miaowing hungrily all night; Anis, who has attached himself to me in Voy's absence, pinching the lamp and begging cigarettes; little Kina's green running nose; the general dilapidation; the inability to separate myself from dirt and animals, the dead rat which lies on the mat when I get up. What is it? I wonder vaguely as I pick it up by its disgusting tail and flick it out into the banana grove. A *ratus sordidus*? Dick Morton would know.

I have finished *Tender Is the Night*. Now I shall work. No more reading. Reading separates me mentally from the place, especially Scott Fitzgerald. It makes me feel alien here, and the people look more like strangers. I think I will go up to Numndi's garden and pretend to work with them—high up on the mountain, where the breezes fan one's face and where you can look silently down through the wafting mists and smoky hills, a garden on top of the world. They will chatter and work, undistracted by its awesome beauty, used to it, digging the soil and making small fires to cook their *kau kau*. And then we will all come down in the evening, me slipping and sliding with my boots, clutching at trees for momentary support, picking my way through the mud; they tripping down daintily and deftly with their axes, knives, *bilums*, and Rafal on Pella's neck, clutching her hair as she grabs him strongly with her left arm. Then I will make the dinner, rice with a smell of meat, and they will tuck into it hungrily while I pick at it, sick of the monotonous taste, and give the rest to Winimp, the dog.

13 August

Rafal started vomiting again yesterday. I'm sure I can see his ribs now. He has lost his double chin and his looks and is pale and tired, still saying 'Hullay' but very weak. And I'm without my little emergency team.

The night was long. Ruminj, with his son Bak, crept in after I had gone to bed, asking if he could sleep here to protect me, pointing out (of course) that *haus Nadya* was full up. I tried politely to deflect him, scarcely feeling like his company for the night, but I was tired and he was determined, so they ended up on Jan's and Mishka's beds. Ruminj coughed and snored all night and went squeaking in and out the door at least eight times.

Finally morning came like a reliable friend, permitting us all to move from our beds of insomnia. Ruminj now tells me he has *pek pek wara*. The place is full of *pek pek wara*. He is sitting outside now being rubbed all over by Moni with large nettle leaves, *nuntz*, the Rulna cure-all. They immediately provoke a huge lumpy rash which he claims will cure him.

Rafal, thank God, is better, rushing from group to group, his 'Hullay' restored to its former vigour, his appetite back to normal. Try as I might, I cannot prevent him from scavenging all sorts of food. He cries for food; they give it to him. With frustrated resignation I hope for the best.

Everyone except the stricken Ruminj and Pella is going to work in Numndi's new garden today, making the fences. In return, they stuff themselves morning and night at his expense—mountains of rice and tinned fish. They won't, he explains to me, work for simple *kau kau*. Now the coffee season is over, they have no money to buy rice, for which they are hungry. Rice is the luxury food, the white man's camp food which has been adopted in the highlands as a prestige dietary item.

By Saturday Numndi's garden will be ready for planting and then the women will take over and plant the vegetables. Pella will have to go. Moni, slender and beautiful, has been working with the men, hacking bush and lugging trees. Numndi continually boasts about her, about her ability to do a man's work. His other helpers are Kints, Anis, Moka, Agena, Dokta and Noki. He will feed them here but with his own rations, all spread out on banana leaves. Now they are preparing food, *kau kau,* for breakfast. The children are *mu-mu*ing a *kapul* which Kints caught in a trap for them. Bak seems to know all the procedures, little as he is: burning the fur, making the hole, lining it with leaves. They made me taste the possum. It tasted sweet, but strange for me—a bit like possum perhaps.

14 August

Now, like a sudden chill wind, the situation has changed. Dokta, they say, is sick and nearly dead, and they must sit and discuss the matter. I suggest that they take him to the *haus sik,* but they shake their heads, saying they doubt if the *haus sik* could help in this case. This, they say, is not *sik bilong haus sik.* This sickness must be treated in the traditional way.

Anyway, they have sent two men to make a stretcher for Dokta and bring him down; meanwhile, they squat on the dust in front of our house with Moka who has brought us the news, all offering, I expect, their own theories on the cause of the illness while Dokta lies helpless.

Agena and Anis have not reappeared with Dokta on a stretcher, and I am debating whether to go and investigate. We can't just let him die. I must try to get him to the *haus sik*. He must have malaria. I know their methods worked for Mishka, but we were going with our system as well. One can't totally rely on the *tipokais*.

Finally they came, without the stretcher, without Dokta, saying that the reason for Dokta's illness having been discovered, he will now recover on his own. Everyone says (and Dokta, it seems, concurs) that he had been angry with Kints, his father, for not giving him some money which Kints had promised him after the Palge had presented him with two pigs in *moka*. Kints, forgetting his promise to Dokta, had given both pigs to old bachelor Wahg, Kints' mate, and had told Dokta that he would get fifty kina, of which only ten had been presented.

Dokta had been harbouring his disappointment and resentment over several weeks, and when he recently reminded his father of the promised debt, Kints grew angry and said, 'I have nothing for you.' So Dokta continued to fume in silence.

Anger with one's close relatives, they explained, is a serious offence when one does not reveal it, and especially if the two parties involved work together, as they had on the Numndi garden project. The ancestral ghost, the *tipokit*, the angry one, takes a very dim view of this duplicitous behaviour and sends immediate punishment in the form of illness and eventually, if the problem is not exposed, death. Anyway, Dokta is better, the ancestors are right, and once again the *redskin* has been proved wrong. So she can go back to her painting.

15 August

Fed up with the general confusion, with being vomited and shat upon for days, and with all the rumours of *plani sik piccaninny* (plenty of sick children), I took my towel, my clothes, my hair and my bedsheets and spent two hours in the river, letting the surging torrent massage me until I felt new, refreshed and cleansed. When I came back I was able to work in my studio, observing and trying to synthesise in my painting the different elements, the changing colours of the green, the leaves, the veiled hills, and the smoky, mysterious distance where Voytek was, somewhere.

In the evening I squatted outside with Numndi, Pella, Moni, Anis and Agena and they talked scary stories; well, scary for them, bizarre for me—stories about snakes and *sangumas* (bush devils).

'A Jimmi man can kill you by taking your stomach and putting leaves and wood in its place.' (Numndi)

'They can change you into a cassowary or a pig, and then you can be killed and eaten. You have become a wild pig.' (Agena)

'We all saw it happen, in Kant, in the Jimmi.' (Anis)

'Who to?' I asked, suddenly anxious and believing more and more in their ridiculous spirits. That's where Voy was going. To Kant.

'He only has to catch your breath to do this.' (Numndi)

'One must never cross a Jimmi man, and never ever let your breath go near him. Jimmi men are *sangumas*.'

'Better not to go there at all, but if he ever gives you anything, then return the gift immediately.'

'But who did it happen to? I mean, in Kant?' I wanted to track down the story, to reassure myself.

'And if you sleep close to a Jimmi man, you won't need a blanket, for Jimmi people have an amazing heat.'

I never did find out who was transformed into a pig and subsequently eaten in Kant. But I found myself wondering if the Jimmi men were aware of how they were regarded here. If they knew they would surely either never come, or else would take over the place, a bloodless conquest, with our hefty Gamegai lying trembling and prostrate in their path.

Now I'm sitting in bed, and outside Moni is teaching Numndi to read pidgin hymns in preparation for his impending Australian tour. I realise now that all white people are seen as missionary types, their function being limited to converting souls and hymn singing.

They come inside for awhile, talking 'scary' again, saying that the way down to the Jimmi can mean instant death.

'The *sanguma* lies waiting. It is a trap set by the Jimmi. One should always cut through the jungle, go around, never by the path.' (Chorus)

They will never get to sleep now, they have all terrified themselves so much, and I probably won't either, thinking about Voytek being stalked by *sangumas*. Looks like another night listening to rat noises.

16 August

Rafal has become a complete insomniac, he woke thirty-five times last night, an average of once every fifteen minutes. In the morning he is sleepy and cranky and so am I. Perhaps he is getting teeth. I don't know. Anyway, the day hardly presents a cheerful aspect. It is dark and raining very softly, so it seems early but probably is not. The shortwave radio won't work for me. It produces a series of drawn-out squeaks, alternating with Japanese language, so I will never know either the time or the news. I have turned it off, frustrated.

I make myself *plour*, a skill which I have developed to a fine art, but I feel sick and can't eat them. I too have got diarrhoea now. *Pek pek wara*. I've given all my medicines to Voy to take with him and to Ruminj. I try the cures in *Where There Is No Doctor*—pawpaw and banana. They don't work.

Rafal, when he was sick, found the thought and the taste of both these cures abhorrent. I feel the same.

Voy, why don't you come home? Then I will be better. I will sleep and so will Rafal, and we can listen to the good old reassuring 'Voice of America' droning out the news in 'special English'. Numndi and all his henchmen have gone up to the garden but they won't work in the rain. So they will come down again. I hope they do; it's kind of lonely here, bleak and desolate.

Numndi says Kunjol, the boy from Tigi, has stolen our yellow blanket. Damn! I wanted to put the two good blankets away for the children. I will be so glad to see their faces again, radiant and excited as we get them off the plane, and the Gamegai will swarm around again, relieved and happy to see their old friends.

Rafal has a small following and he performs for them, dancing and chanting, the chant of the *moka*. They think he is very funny. Perhaps it's the start of his career as a comedian.

Kabuga the cat has killed two rats during the night and left the less tasty parts on the food table. I pour bleach on the table, scrubbing it. But now, hungry again, she steals my *plour*, dragging it away. Furious, I kick her. I'm sick of cats who reproduce themselves and miaow for food, but if she wasn't here we would be overcome by rats and if we fed her she wouldn't catch them. It's a vicious circle. I fill up her milk bowl. That's all she gets.

•

The day turned out quite well after all. The sun did shine and I did a few hours reasonable work. Ruminj came again with gruesome details of his *pek pek wara*. He wanted *redskin* medicine. I listened and tried not to listen. I tried referring him back to his ancestors. He looked at me as though I was mad. Somehow my condition seemed to get worse when I had to hear about Ruminj's symptoms. He told me he had to act as the Village Court Magistrate, Pri and Puruwei from Palge, the usual magistrates, having not turned up at all. Well, I told him, that will be good for your CV when you go for elections.

17 August
My dearest Voy

> I want to just tell you everything that's been happening here right up until tomorrow, when you will come back. It's been a bit difficult without you, apart from the fact that I miss you terribly. It's now raining and misty but we have had a good night's sleep, me and Rafal (he imprisoned firmly in his cot). Numndi managed last night to find Radio Japan for me, with a long-winded program of Australian bush songs followed by elaborate explanations in Japanese. Now the darling has found the morning news for me, albeit the Russian news in English. So one can arrive at some sort of conclusion about what is happening, by convoluting and deducing, subtracting

a bit here and adding a bit there. It's news anyway, a bit different from the news around here, which is mainly pigs, gardens and who is sick.

Radio Moscow waffles pleasantly about the joys of physical culture, how every third Soviet citizen comes to the centre every day for the exercises. Numndi listens solemnly. He wants to check the time with his watch. He shakes his watch. It is not correct, he says sadly. I explain to him that the time on the radio is not our time. But he's still not happy with the watch. I offer to swap it with my mickey mouse model which everyone admires. Numndi has accepted joyfully, not put off by the fact that, as I pointed out to him, this model must be wound every three hours.

He is going up to the garden again today with all his helpers when the rain ceases. Two more days work, then the fences will be finished and the women will go and plant it—such an amazing job, I've been watching it with awe. They just hack into a huge area of forest with their small tomahawks, chopping at the huge trees, heaving the logs, pruning the undergrowth.

I feel a bit overcome when I realise what I am witnessing, this time-honoured slash-and-burn swidden gardening method, and that we won't always be able to look out and see a patch of black stumps on a steep slope, like Druid circles imprinted over the mountainsides. In my heart I realise that it will all disappear into a spot in our memories, and we will tell people that we witnessed one of the most primitive forms of gardening, going back to the Stone Age, and they won't really care because they didn't experience it themselves. But we can talk about it, you and I.

After a couple of weeks, when you're home, it will be green again, but still different from the surrounding bush. It will have all the lush, different greens of the garden, the huge, oval banana leaves, the tapioca, the taro leaves like elephant ears sprouting exotically, and the purple, silver-tinged *kau kau* leaves shining along the ground. Those are all the colours in my head at the moment, as I mix my palette.

Now the voice on Radio Moscow has given place to Prokofiev or Shostakovich—one of those Russians, your neighbours, my darling, a divinely high-flying violin concerto. It sounds like the snow, the rain, troikas. Perhaps I'm being painfully detailed with my writings because you are away and you are my greatest confidant. Now I must commit my days and evenings to paper—easier than painting.

Painting is hard—hard to be satisfied with my work, hard to make progress, to master new techniques so they become unconscious, effortless. I don't like brush marks anymore. I like everything to look fresh, as though it wasn't painted by a hand at all—as though it dropped from the sky, mystically covering the paper like the mists themselves. But the paper is clever, stolid, unable to be deceived, foiling my attempts whenever it can. I will try again now, but first clean the house, find the smells, air the bedding and wash the nappies. It's easy in the river, I don't even need soap. I just hold things in the rushing rapids and rub them against the rocks. They come clean and fresh—well, sort of clean. Rulna clean. Now I'm going to paint.

So to work. But first I shall go to Pella's house to see if Rafal is all right, that he's not eating white mushrooms which appear everywhere on the wood after rain. I have an obsession with them, and I think of Rafal and his dirty face and soft curly head, bare bum and crazy talk. I rush up there quickly to save him. But he is chatting to Pella's children in what they tell me is Melpa dialect. He is squatting by the fire, eating not white mushrooms but *kau kau*.

I mentioned my fear to Pella, pointing out the offending objects of my obsession. She giggled understandingly, sympathetically, feeling, I think, genuinely sorry for me. And then Rafal spotted me and wanted to come back with me. But no, I said, I want to paint now. No, you stay here but don't touch the white mushrooms. He cried. He pulled at my skirt. I disengaged him and walked off trying to look determined. They all stared after me, clutching Rafal who wailed vociferously.

I haven't the heart to write anymore. I just want you to come, but my wish is so strong it makes me feel wretched.

Keep safe for me, my dearest.
Kot

Ah, so now I am back again, in my little studio. I will distract myself. I will paint. But first, I will finish my diary.

Voy, at least, will understand about the white mushrooms, share my fear. He also worried when the python lived under our house and we tied the mosquito net in a big knot under the bottom of Rafal's cot to stop the python getting in with him and strangling him. We had heard, you see, that pythons are attracted to the smell of milk.

'But pythons are harmless! Anyway, if there's no other food around, you can eat them!' Pella was amazed at our attitude towards this benign tenant of our hut.

It was the same with the mosquitoes and the net. When we first came I covered Rafal in a huge net after four-thirty each afternoon, instructing anyone looking after him to do the same.

'Mosquitoes,' I would point out. '*Kit* Rafal!' (No good for Rafal.)

They nodded understandingly and then whisked

off his net, trying it on themselves, peering at the new image in the car mirror.

Professor Forge, Voytek's boss, gave us a green battery-operated gadget which, if one hangs it around the neck, is supposed to repel all the mosquitoes in the area. It is said to emit a secret noise that resembles the mating call of the female mosquito and scares off the malarial types. Or something. Rafal was, in addition to his bridal veil, elegantly encumbered with this device until such time as I realised there weren't actually hordes of mosquitoes to be repelled. Anyway, by this time Rafal had been relieved of his device by hands unknown.

My work is not going well but I blame the paper. It is damp, heavy, uncooperative. And my studio needs a haircut—I can't see out. What a struggle. Perhaps it's like Voy, struggling with English.

'But Kot! *Why* don't you know the meaning of this word?'

'But Voy, I do. This is the meaning.'

'No it isn't, Kot! See here, look in the dictionary!'

'No, Voy. Listen. The dictionary is *wrong, mistaken*, written by an ignorant man. Just listen to me and you'll learn!'

'Nonsense! You don't know your own language. In Polish there are *no* words which I don't know. Why are there so many words which you don't know? This *curva* English! When you were away I ran up the mountain, up to Noki's garden, every day and on the way I memorised six new words, repeating them over and over.'

I try to explain that words need prepositions, conjunctions, a definite article, joining words, little words within which to couch the big words. I encourage him to 'Throw away the dictionary!'

Yes, that's what it's like for Voy with English, and for me too with painting—a struggle which I try to avoid, to forget, but I can't. Back and back I go, and sometimes there's a ray of light, a new step, an illumination, progress. Voy, with all his great ideas, has to push the words through the maze of construction: of colons, of semicolons, wherebys, wherefores, notwithstandings; and, of course, the definite article. Poles can't get it right. Olek was the same: the word 'the' all over the place when it's not needed, and not a trace of one when it's appropriate.

Each paragraph for Voy is a struggle—five cups of coffee and many Polish swear-words. I help, nervous, lest he ask me a word which I don't know again, but in the end it is he who pushes it through, with a great effort, like a whale giving birth. Thinking about him like this makes me suffer, wishing he was here, to have the contact, any sort of contact, even an argument about vocabulary.

We have talked about a word processor. Allan and Francesca have one. It sounds wonderful, better than a typewriter. They produce beautiful work cleanly, efficiently—a blithe couple, not only gifted and good-looking but amusing, fun to be with, especially Allan. He always makes me laugh. We sometimes meet them in Hagen, and we look forward to it. We all dress up, buy wine and go for dinner in the hotel.

Their lives in Nebilya are far more controlled and

ordered than ours, we think guiltily; they have no kerosene fridge, no car. They live on hard chick peas and tinned Chinese duck. We know that because we stayed the night with them and saw all the tins. They opened one for us. It was disgusting by our standards. The bones of the duck were like chalk and the flesh bore no resemblance to duck whatsoever.

Rafal cried incessantly that night at their place, keeping everyone awake. 'What's wrong with him?' they asked, and I just wished that they had a baby and then they would know that we didn't have any answers or solutions, that there was no way in the world of shutting him up, and that there was probably nothing wrong with him at all—he was just being bloody-minded and felt like keeping everybody wide awake all night.

Because they lived near the town, we brought frozen chickens for them, trying to be good guests. The chickens were stolen before we even got into their house. It had never happened to them before. What was it about us? Did we look like a soft touch? Anyway, we paid the price for letting it happen when we were forced to eat their tinned Chinese duck instead of fire-cooked chicken.

At Rulna we bring down frozen chickens in our four-wheel drive and stuff them into the kerosene fridge. We also buy whisky from the Catholic bishop, and occasionally, if we're feeling expansive, a bottle of wine. We hide it all under our bed or down between the bamboo wall mats. We derive great pleasure from meting out our rations at night, sipping our whisky secretly, lying in bed away from peering eyes.

However we discovered that it wasn't such a secret. Once Ruminj found the bottle and shared it out with his mates, replacing it with whisky-coloured liquid with a vile taste. Voy came back after one of his long trips and at night, legs up, decided to have a sip. Fury. What a mean, low-down trick! Ruminj was summoned and immediately admitted, yes, he had taken it and they had all enjoyed themselves very much and, yes, he would give Voy the eight kina for the half bottle. 'But what was the liquid?' Voytek asked, outraged. Ruminj just smiled his toothless smile, amused at the stupidity of the question. It was a perfect colour match, he said. Didn't we agree?

Now I've almost got it—got what I want. But I need a smoke and a walk. The way the yellow light transforms the green, suddenly and subtly; the large, furled leaves of the banana tree, bright against the view, behind which is greyish, not bright but smoky, mysterious. I don't know why I can't paint a flower. Perhaps it will come to me.

Dokta has come, together with a crowd. The crowd sits outside and Dokta, Kongga his wife, and Maga from down the valley sit in our house. I inquire about his recent illness. He tells me that, yes, he was not only nearly dead, he was in fact dead. Everybody was crying, tearing their hair and their beards, keening. He was going down a road he had never seen before, following a warm yellow glowing light, and children were beckoning him. Kongga and Maga nodded solemnly, embellishing the story with their own versions. Then, Dokta says, he slept, and when he awoke he spoke about the evil thoughts boiling inside him and he recovered immediately.

I ask what the great crowd here is about as I start to throw my washing into the back of the house. Crowd time is always steal time; any accumulation of people on the premises means loss of t-shirts, nappies, can-openers, scissors and lamps. The crowd, Dokta explains, is awaiting the arrival of Benjamin Kui, the Gamegai who has made good in Hagen, who works in the bank, who will, they say, drive here in his new car which they have all invested in. Could I cook him some lunch?

'Yes, of course I can. When and if he comes I will boil some rice.' Dokta, his mission of request completed, goes to watch for his investment driving down the road.

All the old men and the bigmen waited on the road, sitting there in the dust, listening for the sound of the engine, playing cards, chewing betel nut, rolling their tobacco, waiting, expectant. Benjamin did not arrive. But the expectation of his coming didn't die. I left the house and went to the mission for my walk, feeling furious with Benjamin Kui for tricking precious money out of his gullible clansmen. I bought a duck and some duck eggs from Brother Paul.

Voy is coming tomorrow and I will have roast duck and even a lettuce which I saved. I haven't had meat since he left, confining myself in his absence to sweet potato, duck eggs and rice. We will feast together on Sunday, tomorrow. Brother Paul gave me some homemade buns, too, and Numndi found the news again tonight. He's a genius—Radio Australia! Many Poles were arrested and injured yesterday during huge riots in Warsaw and Gdansk. It was the second anniversary of Solidarity.

18 August

Sunday has arrived at last, but not without a struggle. There was a huge earthquake last night. The bed rumbled and jumped and rocked from side to side. I clung to the bed and to Rafal, terrified, thinking the world was going to crumble, disintegrate. And then there was another one—oh no. The jars shook on the shelf and something dropped from the shield above my head— my face cream, landing with a sharp bang on my cheek. Anis called out. The whole place was awake, frightened.

I thought of Voy, sleeping in the bush on the bouncing ground. I waited for the sound of trees, houses crashing down but there was none. All was quiet again. I went back to sleep. Morning came, sunny and serene, and everyone talked about the earthquake—the *guria*. They say it's a man who lives under the ground and he has the shakes because he is hungry. They know they should always leave some food for him beside their fires but they keep forgetting to do this. He's a man of the night, the earthquake man; he doesn't come in the daytime—no, never.

Ruminj wants to go to meet Voy with me, to wait at Wara Ilk with greasy *plour*, and this time everybody, including Kints, is excited about the plan. '*Pa!*' he says authoritatively, pointing his axe in the direction of the valley. '*Nim Ruminj Pa!*' Meekly I accept that we should go, although I think to myself that it's wrong, that it could misfire somehow. But Kints' word is law. These rescue parties rarely reach their quarry. There is always another path, a short cut. Besides which, what will happen to the dinner while I'm gone? The roast duck will be burnt, at best. I think I shall suggest Ruminj and Anis instead of me.

They will then stop down below a bridge somewhere and, with the luxurious light of our Coleman lamp, will sit and play cards and relish the cold *plour*. Then they will come home—hurt, surprised, amazed that Voy got here and they didn't find him. Anyway, it is only morning now, we don't know what time. We never do find out the time, Numndi and I, even with the help of our radio. But it is still cool and the shadows are long.

•

I went down to mass. Brother Paul said the earthquake had been on the news—seven on the Richter scale. The mission shield was hanging on its side and the

Blessed Virgin had crashed to the ground. Outside the church there was a young church leader from Tigi, brother of Mikel Kewa, haranguing the crowd, berating all these bush people down here for being lazy, for not having built a proper church, for not having their hearts in these matters. All they care about, he said, is getting more wives and swapping pigs.

He said that around Hagen now there is too much trouble, too many men being killed, too many women carrying on adulterous relationships, too much stealing and crime. If these stupid bush people only knew, they too would settle for Jesus Christ. Others joined in the debate: Dokta and then Ruminj.

I listened in on the conversation, however, and discovered that the topic had switched dramatically. It had switched to pigs. Ruminj, on his feet above the squatting crowd, was castigating anonymous culprits for not finding out which pig had got into his garden and wrecked it. Not a toya of compensation had he received. Others joined, shouting. Kaip, the Rulna church leader, asked by Brother Paul to stop and begin the mass, motioned Brother Paul to wait a little.

Mass began. 'It is the Feast of the Assumption,' Brother Paul explained, delighted to be able to give the sermon in Father Josef's absence. 'Our Lady never went rotten in the cemetery, she came out, went to heaven and stands with twelve stars on her head and the moon below her right foot.'

All the Gamegai must ask her intercession if things go wrong, he said. If they need help. Besides which, it is Vocation Sunday. More priests are needed—native priests, not white men. It is a serious situation when the whole of independence has spread everywhere except to the church. 'Why are there no black priests? Why are we running out of nuns too, and catechists?'

Outside, Ruminj was still under the tree grumbling about his pig, arousing a moderate amount of interest and excitement over his grudge.

On the way home, I was accosted by John Moka Palge, who told me his son had been gravely ill for the last week and was on a drip. He then went on to say that he was deeply concerned because all the court magistrates and he, the Clerk of the Court, wanted a lift to Hagen tomorrow to the Supreme Court for the hearing concerning Numndi, Menzeli the dog and Gabriel Kei, the storekeeper. I had thought that was all over.

Incredulously, I checked with Numndi, who concurred—Gabriel Kei was counter-suing him over the dog Menzeli incident and had Father Josef's backing. I now fear for Numndi that white justice might triumph, that the person attacked by the dog might be the victim and victor in this case. Then Numndi would have to pay dearly. Numndi is far from worried. He looks more sage than ever. He is convinced that all the local magistrates will be on his side, that he will be the one extracting even further compensation.

18 August
My dearest Voy

Night-time. I waited for you, Voy, and you didn't

come. I am still writing and peering into the darkness, but Ruminj has returned now and it's nine o'clock and you didn't turn up at the river crossing. Ruminj, Mikel Kewa and Dokta waited for you with supplies and lamps. Graciously they returned them to me and I fed them. They are still here chatting to Numndi who has hurt his foot and poles himself along on a long stick, like a gondoliero without a gondola.

I still have the duck I bought to celebrate your return. I kept it for you, wrapped in blankets. We shall eat it tomorrow. I can make it hot again. I feel flat after my excitement of waiting, but I know what can keep one in the bush here: broken bridges, swollen rivers, a sore foot or just sheer distance, a thousand things really. Better not to think about them, better to go to bed. I hope you sleep all right out there in the bush my darling—I shall walk to meet you tomorrow.

19 August

It is such a beautiful day today; fresh, sunny. I think of you walkers already having walked for three hours, now probably somewhere in the forest between here and the Jimmi. Ruminj wants to go again to meet you and cook breadfruit at Wara Ilk, waiting. He has stopped irritating me now. He looks noble again and is charming enough, too. His red teeth with the big front gap used to worry me, but one gets used to red teeth and gaps.

Ruminj has been very attentive to me. The other night I was getting up to go to the toilet and there was Ruminj, outside the hut, bush knife raised in anticipation of a rascal. I actually got quite a fright until I realised who it was. He is protecting me while you are away. His presence in *haus Nadya* is definitely reassuring. Ruminj always makes you bristle and I get the feeling that you irritate him in the same way— you grate on each other. You must be similar types; well, not necessarily, I'm just raving.

Night falls, and I prepare the homecoming feast again. Once more Ruminj turns up alone, bringing back the supplies. He and Kongga went this time, and Kewa too. They say they will go tomorrow. Time is hanging heavy and I feel dragged down by disappointment and uncertainty. If you don't come tomorrow or the day after that I shall have to pull myself out of this state, eat the bloody duck and not prepare homecoming feasts any longer. Then I could work again or at least try. I shall let the sheets get dirty and the house get filthy and eat all the remaining food (which is only the duck anyway) and then you will come.

Numndi tells me sagely that a watched pig never fattens. Numndi, Pella and Moni are always here now. Numndi's sore leg prevents him from going to his garden, so he stays here with me and his women. He was even working a *bilum* today, fingers flying as deftly as any woman's. We sat together at the river and ate *marita* and talked nonsense, played with Rafal and cooked bread-fruit on the fire. I can hear him practising his hymns now, for Australia. Goodnight, Rulna, and goodnight my Voy, wherever you sleep.

Kot

20 August

So now I've stopped waiting I can operate again. I've switched myself and am in another gear. Everyone agrees with me.

Rafal is healthy and fat once more. He is crazy about Greta, Numndi's daughter, and follows her everywhere, crowing and calling 'Hullay'. Yesterday she jammed her fingers in the car door and then Numndi, to comfort her, clouted her over both ears. She sat in the dust, crying and lamenting, her tears turning the dust to mud.

Rafal stood looking at her, genuine concern in his eyes, then he knelt and put his head on her lap. She kept wailing, uncomforted, so he brought some things, putting them next to her; small stones, a rotten lemon. Still she sobbed, unheeding. Rafal then gave up, shrugged his shoulders and wandered off.

It turned out, Numdi was right—the hearing

ended up exactly as he said it would. Gabriel Kei had to pay Numndi two more pigs, despite the presence of the formidable Father Josef, as the key witness, saying that the man bitten by the dog should be the one to receive compensation.

Anis is sick with a *het i pen na skin ut tu* (headache and temperature) but he wants to take part in the evening ceremony, the going-to-meet-Voytek, which is becoming a daily event involving three constants: Kewa, Ruminj and, for some mysterious reason, Kongga. Also Agena and Anis. They take the 'supplies'—they insist on this even though they don't venture more than two hours' walk away—of raisins, walnuts and smokes. Each night they return them to me, intact, with the lamps, and then wait for their dinner.

Before leaving this time, Anis performed his own small bit of magic. He lit a long, upright coil of paper, the inside paper from a packet of Cambridge cigarettes, and waited to see whether the ash went up or down. If it went up, he explained to me with a straight face, Voy would come. If it went down, Voy would not come. It went down. Anis shook his head, pondering whether to cancel his mission. I encouraged him to go off anyway, telling him that should Voy come he might be very weak by the time he gets to Wara Ilk, and the extra nourishment might save his life. They went.

It is *kapiac* (breadfruit) season. All day long they make fires and cook the breadfruit and then sit shelling the segments and eating them, feeding bits to Rafal who has his mouth permanently held open in expectation, like a small bird.

The ownership of the breadfruit trees is suddenly called into question as one family picks off one tree and another clan member claims it as his, citing as proof long rigmaroles of descent and succession which can go anyway according to who feels stronger and more hungry, or so it seems to me.

My darling

So, Voy, you're not going to come. Anis's paper said so, and I suddenly lost my vision of you striding, sweating and single-minded, through the bush, homeward bound. You are somewhere in the Jimmi still, behind all those cloudy mountains, feasting on festive pig or watching some initiation ceremony and feeling removed from us all here, absorbed in your project, oblivious to me, who waits for you.

In two days Nadya will be fifteen. If you're not home, I will have to go to Hagen to ring her up. I really must talk to her on her birthday.

Numndi won twelve kina at cards today (beginning with two, he told me) and solemnly handed six to me, making a small speech about why he was driven to this generosity.

'You are without your *redskin* man, and we can see that you have no money and no food.

We, however, are not going to let you starve while he is away.'

But there is never 'no food' here. There is breadfruit—the trees are laden heavy; there is *kau kau*, bananas. They cook food all day long and carefully dole out my ration. Rafal will never be in any danger of starving—Rafal the scavenger, the *redskin* baby with his white hair. His stomach protrudes indecently, impeding his walk. He has learned to do a very funny thing, I've noticed. He does a poo on the ground, squats to contemplate it, and then goes and covers it with dirt, digging around it with a stick. Do you think that could be called potty training? Anyway, it's not a pleasant thing to step on one of those disguised shits.

Ruminj has borrowed one of your shirts and a sarong. Tomorrow he wants to go to the Mabege country to canvass votes for the position of Village Court Magistrate. Unfortunately for his chances, it seems that at least ten other men are standing for this position.

Goodnight, my darling. I've stopped waiting for you in the acute sense, but my heart still waits, more quietly now.

Kot

But this time the paper prophecy was wrong. I went down to the mission to buy some eggs and who should I see coming out of the advancing gloom but a white man with a pack. I had reached such a stage of resignation that I thought it was a mirage, or someone else. But there, yes, there he was, my own *redskin*, accompanied by Councillor Kuk, who was carrying a huge cassowary trussed up in a long cage, its disdainful head protruding from the end. Voy all right—very slim, very dirty.

Mission forgotten, eggs forgotten, I rushed down the hill to meet him and then we just stood there for a moment, looking at each other. Kuk stopped too, and the cassowary turned its head to peer at me, its opinion lost in its inscrutable black gaze. That's how we met, after all that waiting. Then we just walked together up towards our hut, quite shy, hardly saying a word, and were gradually surrounded by onlookers. Still silent, after those weeks of living so much within myself, I regenerated the feast that I had been saving and hiding, that poor old duck, its off taste lightly disguised by wild chilli and ginger.

Voy looked light, like an old photograph of himself in Rangoon. Even his arms were thin. I had some difficulty approaching this new person. I had to feed him, to bring him back into the present. He was exhausted and excited. He had just returned from another land, the land beyond the distant forests. His head was somewhere else. I had to reclaim him.

I had been living in my territory, he in his. He wouldn't have spoken a word of English in weeks, or even thought in English. He was getting his grammatical constructions wildly wrong. His mind was exhausted, but racing from whatever events he had just been witnessing. We went to the river and washed, sitting under the cool, gushing water. Then he lay down on the bench on our verandah while I cooked.

Numndi looked at him lying motionless and started to mutter about the *sanguma*.

'Oh Numndi, shut up about the stupid *sanguma*. He's just tired and starving. It's hunger. And thirst.' I would never convince Numndi.

21 August

The night was ours, but this morning he gave me the shock.

'I have to go back.'

'What?'

'Yes. There are initiation ceremonies next week at Tsandiap. I can't miss them.'

I was amazed. I couldn't even argue. I had just got used to him, sitting, having coffee. His skin felt warm and dry. It was the two of us again. I was enjoying his strange boyish thinness. And now, for him to leave me for some ridiculous reason, to strand me again with my difficult thoughts—it seemed unthinkable.

But, I told myself, I have learned my independent woman artist routine now; I will learn to like it more. Who needs men anyway? And now, with Anis's paper trick, I won't even have to make too many unnecessary feasts. So just go, will you! First, though, this condition: we go to Hagen to ring Nadya for her birthday and get supplies.

23 August

It was Nadya's birthday yesterday. She was fifteen. We never got to Hagen. I couldn't phone her.

My dearest Nadya

> It's your birthday and I'm not with you. I feel completely helpless, trapped here without any chance of getting to town to even ring you up. I can hardly even say I'm sorry, because I know that this is where you want to be anyway, and that you probably blame me. But I am sorry, I'm sad, and I feel I've let you down.
>
> So, my dearest girl, happy birthday! I hope it's a very happy birthday. I know Jan will make you a cake, and Mishka will make a speech, and David will step into his role once again as godfather and make a party.
>
> Could it be true that you were born fifteen years ago? When you were little you didn't want to celebrate any birthdays because you said you didn't want to be older. Now, when I measure our lives since that time in terms of events I think you could be fifty. So much drama, so many places. And at fifteen, to have already lost your

father four years before, you do have that sad spot in your soul, but you can always turn sadness to creativity with your great spirit.

Do you remember your fourteenth birthday, and the bra theft? This place is sometimes so bizarre and somehow we get caught up in the strangeness of the events. The only thing I can do for you now is to keep you informed.

That young girl Pella—you know, that really annoying one from the Kawelka tribe at Tigi—she's been staying with Numndi and she became very sick in his house. We carried her to the *haus sik* and paid her *haus sik* tax. No-one else was going to pay it. I don't think they wanted her to go there. No doubt there are other plans afoot for her cure. Pacifying and feeding the ancestors.

And then last night, almost as I watched her, Timb's baby died. You know Timb, that tall, quiet man who lives right up on the mountain top behind our house? You know, the ones you gave the kittens to, and you gave his wife Palg a rather good bracelet for her baby girl? The baby and the worried parents visited yesterday, looking for Dokta Miki. The baby looked desperate, way beyond Dokta Miki's competence even if he were here, so I quickly sent them down to the *haus sik*. But the baby died before they got there. And then they returned with the dead baby, stopping at our place to get a little Rafal blanket to wrap it in. And I became involved in their tragedy.

Voy and I struggled up the hill in the dark, taking our pathetic offering of rice and cigarettes. That's what Numndi told us to do. It didn't seem to me as if it would help at all. 'They must all have hard work to do, crying,' he said, therefore visitors must bring them food and smokes. When we entered their hut, they were sitting round the fire in the dark house, wailing and crying softly, the way they do here. Timb was holding his dead baby wrapped in a blanket with Palg crouched next to him. We placed our offering in the heap of other gifts and sat for awhile with them. Then we crept out, feeling so sorry for them, and inadequate to help. We just left them to their grief. Today everyone is sad, and tired after crying all night.

I gave them some wood to make a small coffin and one of Rafal's blankets, feeling revulsion and fear myself that one could lose one's precious baby. Numndi and Ruminj will bury her. The parents are never expected to perform this last sad task.

Hey, this is supposed to be a birthday letter and I'm going on and on about a dead baby! Sorry!

Voy went again in the early grey morning, laden with cameras and tape-recorders. He took only your Agena this time. Agena, as you can imagine, was not that keen on going, he was muttering about the *sangumas*. But Numndi talked him into it for Voy's sake. They don't know when they will come back.

Voy has had malaria and is now a thin person. You can no longer call him 'Fatty'. He's lost, I would say, twenty kilograms. Kints says to Voy: 'If you go you will die.' Very reassuring for me, feeling as I do, somehow flat, indecisive and full of grey cold mists, like the early morning here. I really miss you and the boys. Everybody does.

Now that the baby has died, groups of villagers meet everywhere, discussing the reason for her death. Palg must have been with another man, they say, and they have nominated Dokta, of all people, as the adulterer. I mean, can you imagine Dokta? With that great big Palg? I know for a fact that it was pneumonia. I saw the baby. But nobody takes any notice of me.

Anyway, Dokta has shut himself into your house and says he is seriously ill himself. I gave him some medicine, trying things my way. I'm attempting to bolster a few frightened spirits against this nervous period. They huddle around me as if I'm a shelter. The problem is, I don't feel so secure myself. I can't even drive out of here. The responsibility is almost overwhelming.

I think about home often now, and about how this strange life here must affect your whole future. You will always have it with you, inside you, colouring your decisions, your behaviour. I would give anything at this moment to be back in our house together. It would be freezing winter. The frosts would be icing the paddocks in front of our house, the sky would be heavy with distant snow, the horses would have their winter coats. The fire in the living room would be making the house sparkle. You would all be sitting around it, warming your bums. I would be preparing your birthday party.

For sure you would disagree with me about wanting to go home, and would just want to stay here in Rulna forever, tending baby pigs and paying compensation for crimes you never committed, being bossed around by those stupid ancestors. I think of Olek, up there, fussing around, trying to influence and educate the other ancestors, scoring the occasional victory. I actually thank God for the time he spent here as a medical patrol officer. Some of those other ancestors he would have even met and done favours for. There are a few up there who would owe him one. That's good for us, and for Numndi and Pella.

Every time we eat we either share our rations with fifteen people or else we sit choking on our dinner while they stand or sit around staring at us. I approach my meals now as I would a battleground, preparing the timing, the place, the tactics, bracing myself for the inevitable internal struggle: to be mean and choke on my own; to share and go hungry; to rudely chase everyone away. But it's no good, a new group would appear immediately. They must like my cooking!

24 August

Rafal woke—before dawn. I was reading till late and was in no way ready to get up, but unbeknown to me I had visitors. Ruminj suddenly materialised from behind the house and bore Rafal away, delighted that someone else was awake to keep him company. He asked for a smoke, I gave him four and gratefully drifted back into my lost sleep. This morning—it is morning now—it is sunny.

But there is still plenty of trouble. This young girl Pella is still very sick. Her father, Merl, has come down from Tigi, and if one imagined he might be a little grateful for the care and money bestowed on his daughter, one would be wrong. He is saying that she is sick because of Numndi's neglect—because Numndi is her host (even though nobody actually invited her here, she just came). Notwithstanding the fact that the *haus sik* fees have been paid for from our pockets (Numndi's, as he understands it), he is now raising hell, saying that everybody must buy a duck or a pig and give it to *tipokai*. Then and only then will she get better. *Tipokai* is cross with them all. God I get sick of *tipokai*.

Of course Mikel Kewa strongly recommends this line of action, saying, yes, *haus sik* medicine will help but will not 'win' the sickness.

Merl exhorts the brothers to buy pigs, saying that when the girl gets married to Casper Penggi (that is the plan, it seems) they will all be repaid in brideprice for their contributions. If, on the other hand, she loses her sanity because of the failure of her uncles to provide the medicinal sacrifice, they will miss out on the brideprice, for Casper Penggi will no longer want her.

Convinced by this argument, they still have not managed to raise a toya for the pigs. They say they have put all their money into buying this car from Ben Kui the entrepreneur—you know, the educated one who works at the bank in Hagen? This despite the fact that not one person in the region has a driving licence.

Now Numndi is sick. He has had diarrhoea for two days. He says it's because they ate the pig leg which Kints brought for them, and they didn't offer it to *tipokai*. (Offer the smell, that is. As you know, they always eat the meat themselves.) My view is that he's sick from eating it himself, *tipokai* or no *tipokai*. Having seen that blackened and dismembered pig lying on banana leaves in the sun for hours, I'm surprised that it hasn't made everyone sick. I have given him Lomotil, hoping that this will work despite his convictions to the contrary and thus deflecting another attempt by the greedy *tipokai* to collect another feast for himself.

Dokta, at any rate, seems to have recovered. He, Kongga, and his sister-in-law have been staying here for four days now with their baby pig. I really like that little family. They are gentle and diffident by normal standards, not imposing, and help with small things. Kunjil (the boy from Tigi), inspired by a set of schoolwork I gave him, does sums, exercises by the hour, and I have to correct them. Trouble is, I'm not sure whether they're right or wrong myself, especially at night when I'm sleepy. Maths, as you know, is not my thing. I've never been big on helping with maths homework. Still, we have to try to help him to get into the Kotna school before we leave.

25 August

Today the girl is still sick and now the Rokembo (Kints' family) have finally come up with four pigs and two ducks towards her health. I gave an extra duck so there are three altogether. Kints has given a big pig, Numndi a medium one, Dokta and Moka baby pigs. These two little pigs are strung up in a tree waiting for their slaughter and Kints is making a speech about the gift to *tipokai*. Moka is preparing to kill the pigs. Mungga, the girl's uncle, speaks and Numndi translates for me.

'We must give these pigs to God because Satan has made Pella sick, and we must talk the truth about why she is sick, who has done wrong.'

I know it's *tipokai* they are addressing, not God. Who does Numndi think he's fooling? They say it was Merl at fault, the father. But he only gave one duck. Surely if it was his fault he should be the main giver. They wanted four from him but he couldn't quite raise the money.

Now John Moka Palge's baby has died. It was brought back to the *haus sik* last night and the *dokta boy* said there was nothing he could do. This morning it died, also from pneumonia.

Pella from Tigi is still not better. They say she 'calls out' everybody's names, and they are worried because already the pigs and ducks have not worked so now they start to think of poison and antidotes. Cassowary shit and the vomit of a bat are the suggested remedies for this stage of the illness, when pigs and ducks fail. Remember this when you say you want to live here. Cassowary shit when you're feeling shit.

26 August

Today Pella is better and there is a bit of jubilation around the place. My opinion, which I don't share with anyone, is that the girl decided to recover rather than face another dose of bat vomit. Numndi too is better. The girl and her family have gone back to Tigi, satisfied at last with the solicitous treatment which their daughter received at the hands of their Rulna hosts. No stone had been left unturned in the search for her cure. They have given the big pigskin and the head of the pig to Mungga, to take to Tigi as a sign of the strengthening of goodwill between the two tribes

Dokta has recovered enough to be engaged in 'courting' the family who have spread malicious rumours about his involvement with the big woman Palg, the mother of the dead baby. He and Kongga, Mepa and the baby pig are still sleeping here in your room. Pri came tonight to gossip to me in my lonely cooking vigil. He likes to moan about his problems. Once again his wife has left him. He says he's fed up with women, the way they think, the way they act, and his sister is with him looking after his children and his pigs and that's enough women for him. The next wife he finds, he says, has got to be the hard-working kind—no more of this other nonsense.

He's just been up in Kotna trying to retrieve Pig's wife for him—another humbug, he says. He's fed up with being a court magistrate and would like to turn over the job to Ruminj and catch his breath a bit, sit around the place for awhile doing nothing—*siddun noting*.

Guess what! Three young Germans were brought to me this morning by some Mabege.

They had found them completely lost and desperate in the bush, miles away from anywhere. Supposedly they had set off for a hike from the Baiyer Road some days before. They had wanted to detour via bush tracks. They almost cried when they saw me, a white woman, here in the bush, and can you imagine how amazed I was to see them? Two nights and one day they stayed here with me, recovering from their ordeal, and then I arranged a lift for them with a coffee truck.

Okay my dearest fifteen-year-old daughter, I can't wait to see you running down the track again; all of you, in fact. We all wait for you. Please look after yourself. Kisses to the boys.

Love, Mum

26 August

So now I am alone again here, the *redskin meri*, pottering around, occupying myself harmlessly but, I think, usefully, painting a bit, reading, emerging and withdrawing back into the secluded darkness of the hut. Rafal visits me from time to time, strutting, stomach in the forefront, with cheerful aplomb, surrounded by his cohorts. We all talk now about the others, the big children. Two more weeks to go and then they come back. Everybody has great plans. They want to see them get off the plane.

watched by ancestors

But now the cheerful climate has turned again. There is deep concern about Dokta and they all sit discussing him. It seems that Palg's family will take him to court. Kints is here to discuss the matter and to sleep the night in Mishka's bed, to protect me with his bush knife. He will cough and snore all night and get up at dawn, and keep the lamp on all night to ward off the *tipokits* (bush spirits), but I am touched at his gesture of gallantry.

27 August

But that did not happen. It is now Friday morning, court morning. Kints was dragged from his bed in the middle of the night. People were rushing around with lights, calling and shouting. Rafal eventually awoke too, shouting, so I went to borrow a light and see what all this fuss was about. There was a big talk going on in *haus Nadya* where Dokta is sleeping.

Kints had been summoned. Pati, Palg's brother, was there with his fellow accusers. The case was already under way. Dokta denied all charges and his brothers stuck by him steadfastly. Now the court will go all day and find its verdict. Either Dokta must win and receive compensation for loss of his good name or else the mother of the dead child must get compensation from him. There can be no stalemate.

Another case being heard is Rot's 'divorce' from the plain *meri bilong wok* with whom, they say, he never slept—an angry young woman, altogether different from Maria, the saucy widow who is now heavy with Rot's child.

Rather than sit around court all day in the dust I shall stay here, quiet, with everybody occupied elsewhere, and paint. They will come back later and tell me the findings, when the shadows begin to lengthen. I feel sorry for the mother, Palg, if in addition to losing her baby she has to pay with all her pigs. On the other hand, it is obvious to me that Dokta is a most unlikely adulterer.

Now I wonder what will come out of the death of John Moka's baby? Certainly the mother will not be left to grieve in peace. She will be blamed somehow and will have to pay compensation to someone. The death of a baby here must indicate a transgression on the part of the mother. But perhaps that makes her feel better; the fact that she can give a few pigs may relieve her feelings of utter helplessness in the face of death. The guilt is taken away from her and transformed into material goods, one way or another. In our society a mother grieves for months, even years, suffering nebulous feelings of guilt at her possible role in causing the death of her child, yet nobody would ever blame her to her face. Thus she can't fight back, can't expiate her hidden guilt and her doubts. She must struggle with her feelings alone.

Our society turns its face away from death; this society faces it squarely and deals with it in a way received and understood by everybody. In the old days, before the *kiaps* came, the parents cut off their fingers at the knuckles, one for the death of each child. Now they don't do that, but they tear their hair and beards, they wail, they follow a prescribed routine.

Now evening approaches. The Dokta case has raged on and off for most of the day. He has been found guilty and ordered to pay one pig—a huge pig. He indignantly refused, saying they were lying with the accusation that he had slept with the woman Palg and that he will not pay as much as one mouse to her. He is furious and will take no notice of the decision. He will go to a higher court and, if necessary, prison.

Numndi, Moka and Ruminj all support him, saying that the court magistrates are hungry for some pig meat. Policeman Mai came down from Tigi to help with the case, saying, on the side, that he wants to build up his reputation a bit and stand for magistrate, a rival for Ruminj. That means guests for dinner I expect—what a drag. Perhaps I shall tell them I'm *sik mun*. (Here, if a woman cooks for her family while menstruating—*sik mun*—she can poison all of them.) What a splendid idea.

I just saw Mikel Kewa carrying a huge branch of red chillies. Curious, I asked him what he wanted to do with them. Despite the abundance of chillies growing around here, I have never heard of anyone using them. His pig, he explained, still has an infected wound from an axe blow, and he must mix the chillies together with tinned fish and kerosene to make a healing balm for the wound.

'Some balm!' I exclaimed. 'It must be extremely *un*soothing!'

Then I asked him why, as he is the *dokta*, did he not use a topical antibiotic.

'Me no savvy,' he replied, and trotted off with his chillies.

Oh, now another turn of events. Dokta's outrage, it seems, has borne fruits. A visiting magistrate and the policeman Mai from Tigi have tried the case again and now the charge against Dokta has been defeated. It seems that if the defendant is strong enough in pleading innocent it is taken as a sign that he should be exonerated. But Palg, the grieving mother, has not been exonerated; it is presumed that she must have been with somebody else. She has to pay her husband ninety kina for the loss of his baby.

I, they warn, can expect a visit from Councillor Kongga from Tigi. He has come down for the court case and expects a present from me. A present for what reason? I inquire. 'Me no savvy,' they answer mysteriously. But I know what it is. He is expecting his hospitality in Tigi to be acknowledged. Fair enough. He gave us his house and was very kind to us. Nothing we have left now would make a present by my standards; our clothes are rags. Perhaps cigarettes would do. A portrait? I could try that.

28 August

Passed without event. I worked all day doing drawings and paintings of Pella and Moni, and a portrait of Councillor Kongga. I had been painting his wife and baby, but he had motioned her away, replacing himself as my sitter. Kongga has come with a list of requests, including one for Voytek's boots. Well, that is the present he wanted. I might have known it wouldn't be a portrait. There is a real waiting list for all of our boots when we leave.

Maliciously, I told him he had better ask Voytek himself if he was really interested in acquiring his boots. 'Old Polish saying,' I warned him. '"Don't divide the skin of the bear before it has even been killed."' (But I substituted 'pig' for 'bear'.) He laughed and slapped me jovially on the shoulder.

29 August

Once again I arose as the red dawn streaked briefly across the dark mountains. Kints, too, got up from Jan's bed, and my maths student, Kunjil. They made a fire and Rafal squatted beside it making his usual conversations.

But now the news has broken out that the charge against Dokta was actually a plot, hatched by Panna the policeman and Timb the father of the dead baby, to extract compensation from Dokta's clan. They would not be able to pay, thus ending up in prison, whereupon Panna and Timb would become our close brothers by default and derive all the mixed benefits (lifts to Hagen etc.) which our former brethren had previously enjoyed. The expounder of this story is Timb's sister, Kunjol, the wife of Yiap. Numndi is delighted beyond description and is now about to take the errant policeman and the bereaved father to court to extract the last of their pigs, money and respect—a gleeful revenge; the triumph of the righteous.

30 August

Voy is coming home tonight so the day will fly for me, preparing the meagre feast and shaking out the blankets. All my guardians will return to their own houses when Voy comes and the quiet will descend once more at night. I won't have to try to sleep in close proximity to coughing men who keep their kerosene lamps on all night to guard against the nocturnal wanderings of their ancestors.

31 August

Voy came home, only a day late. My writings cease for a few days; so does my work. We try to hide in here, in our room. It is not easy. Privacy is an unknown concept around here; however, now and again our observers repair a few metres down the track where they continue to smoke, spit red, foaming betel nut juice and play cards.

Dokta has been calling round every morning to

have his leg dressed. He cut his leg with an axe, but believes the accident was caused by the ancestral spirit of Ping's first husband, Ruk, the one before Ruminj. He said Ruk had been angry at him for contributing towards Ruminj's compensation payments when Ruminj had an affair with Pati's wife, during which they were sprung. Ruk (the spirit) had been furious at Ruminj's shabby treatment of his one-time widow, Ping. Well, those ancestors are certainly kept busy.

Dokta started chatting, too, about his recent 'death', as he termed it. He was very impressed by the whole process: the road, the children pulling him into spirit life and then telling him he must go back when he was nearly there; his family standing over him, crying and wailing, pulling their hair and beards; and then the way he had thrown off his illness by '*outim*' his festering resentment. Failure to do this, he explained, would have meant death, within one day.

3 September

Now, in this totally illiterate society, our typewriter has been stolen. And yesterday our can-opener, again. Pella can open cans with her bush knife, but I can't. It just makes one more level of dependency. When we report the theft, everyone expresses their shock. And that is that. It does not bring back the can-opener.

Ruminj came to Hagen with us yesterday and on

the way back we bought about twenty fish from a boy who was dangling them from a bit of bamboo, near the Kotna River. Upon returning, we gave them to Ruminj to *mu-mu* for everybody. I gave him some rice to cook as well.

'There,' I said to Voy as we sat quietly eating our own small dinner by the light of the candle. 'See how happy everybody is making a *mu-mu*? That must be the price of privacy. It really is worth it!'

We were pleased with ourselves, with our generosity, and mainly with our ingenuity. At which point Ruminj emerged, coming in from the darkness. 'Can you give me something to mix with the rice?' he said

'But Ruminj, you have all those fish!' I cried, amazed.

'But Keti,' he rejoined, 'we have eaten all the fish. Now we want tin fish to put with the rice!'

'RUMINJ!' roared Voytek. 'No more!'

Ruminj was alarmed, surprised, even angry. The two of them turned on each other, eyes blazing. Ruminj retreated to his fire, Voytek to my side. Two angry men.

14 September

At last, the event that everybody had been anticipating, talking about and preparing for: the children's homecoming. And what a homecoming it was. They tumbled out of the plane, Jan and Mishka dressed as the Marx brothers and wearing moustaches. From the first time that they had seen a Marx brothers film, they had become their fervent fans. Mishka had started to see himself as Harpo, and Jan could do a very good Groucho, with his wisecracks and his walk. People even called Mishka Harpo, and it seemed to suit him. When the children heard that Groucho had died, Nadya went to school in mourning.

We were all so happy, laughing all day, hugging each other. Nadya looked ravishing, with shining eyes, the sun in her long hair, and a new slim little body I had not seen before. She looked positively elegant in a white blouse and brown corduroy suit from the Cairns St Vincent de Paul, high-heeled shoes and brightly coloured earrings cascading from her one pierced ear. Heavens, is this what fifteen means? Is this woman my daughter?

The previous day Voy and I had been to a huge funeral feast at Kotna. Men were everywhere, their bulging muscles shining beneath straw bracelets, marching, aggressive, the pigs' skins slung between them on poles, their head feathers making them look tall. I tried to find a place to stand in the marching, surging torrent, but they pushed me out of their way and I fell onto the slippery pig skins lying in careful lines on the ground. I went for a great skid, legs up, bum down, right across the hides. The women all doubled up laughing but the men were angry. I had contaminated the pig meat because I was a woman.

They asked me for money, but I beat a hasty

retreat, smiling nervously and backing off the *sing sing* ground into the bushes. I found Voy, towering whitely above the coloured heads, and stuck close to him. Even so, it wasn't easy to find a safe place to stand. Arms crooked above their decorated heads, women surged up the sloping ground, whole pig hides on their backs, necks heavy with beads.

Puruwei Kuri, the local member of parliament, raced up and down through the throng in his truck, shouting through a megaphone, his driver tooting the horn. The air was thick with dust, and the smell of the 3000 cooked pigs.

Finally the heat, dust and the noise became too much for me. Rafal had dust in his eyes and hair. Coke was no longer quenching our thirst. We escaped to the Watts' home, Ulya, and sat beneath the shady awning of the balcony. Suddenly we were washed and in clean clothes, sipping tea from delicate china cups with the Watts', who were graciously warm and welcoming. Voy and I had a room with a double bed and a pretty bathroom with oils, colognes and mirrors. We were holidaying in a secret resort and the children were coming in the morning. My heart was full of pleasant anticipation.

That night it rained heavily, pounding into the gutters, and I imagined the *sing sing* ground, deserted once more, the wet banana leaves lying in sodden heaps, the *mu-mu* holes filling with water. I hoped the children's plane would arrive safely through the rain.

So now we are back at Rulna and everything is

just as it always was: Voy with his early-morning grumps, Nadya drifting around in red silk drapes, me making *plour,* Jan making dinner, and Mishka chatting seriously with the old men in his typically contemplative manner. We have been told that Voy's typewriter has been appropriated by a man living up the mountain, whom nobody will name. All they can tell us is that he is using it as a pillow. Perhaps it is a softer repose for the head than the usual pillow, which is a log, but I doubt it. One thing I do know now: we will never discover who has this new-fangled pillow, and we will never see our typewriter again.

15 September

Voytek took the children for a long hike up to the mountain tops. They were trying to locate the typewriter. They came back singing. Nadya was marching ahead, her voice blazing their arrival through the misty rain, Rafal was asleep on Voy's back. They brought water in bottles from the little underground spring which spurts like a tap out of the mountain. But no typewriter.

I had been working in my studio, dark in the rainy afternoon, feeling apprehensive about my whole family up on the mountain tops with a storm approaching. I kept glancing up at the black clouds and wincing with every thunderclap, remembering the three pigs that were struck, and the storeman's mother. But Voy and the children had sheltered in an abandoned house on the mountain ridge until the storm rolled over.

Later, towards evening, a big fight took place outside our house. Numndi was escorting a young woman whom everybody said was a *pamuk meri* (whore) up the path towards his home. Pella, who had got wind of this development, was secretly lying in wait for him, crouching behind the large rock in front of our house with a stick hidden inside her dress. Upon meeting them, she whipped out the stick, pretending to shake the woman's hand, and started to beat her husband's new girlfriend, whacking her about the head. She then took the girl by the hand and, with one simple martial arts gesture, threw her over the giant rock into the bushes.

Numndi hit Pella on the nose, making it bleed. Pella picked up a rock, poising it above the weeping girl's head. Then Dokta intervened, gently extracting the rock from Pella's hand. At which stage Voytek, showing his usual degree of anthropological detachment, rushed in, seized the advancing Numndi by the scruff of his neck and threw him. He then took Pella by the arm, offering all the warring parties a smoke. Kongga (the councillor, not Dokta's wife) was Numndi's sole supporter.

Numndi nevertheless managed to take the *pamuk meri* to their house for the night. Pella sat, squatting and sulking. The *pamuk meri* sidled along beside the door, her lap-lap pulled closely around her shoulders. Nadya and Numndi were sitting uncertainly between them, insulting each other. Nadya, I noticed with approval, seemed to be expressing female solidarity with Pella, although I couldn't understand a word she was saying.

16 September

A terrible day, starting with a grey, drizzling dawn which maintained its monotonous momentum throughout the day. Numndi lay skulking in his house with the girl and his wife, who has resorted to bashing both of them from time to time with her stick. And then, as the rain got heavier and the mud thicker, we heard that the *pamuk meri* had left, walking off into the rain.

Mishka decided to go and congratulate Numndi on the outcome of the love triangle. He came back to say that Numndi was lying semiconscious beside his fire, mumbling incoherently.

Those bloody ancestors again, this time threatening the life of our beloved Numndi. We sent Dokta Miki back with the thermometer and he returned saying Numndi's temperature was over forty degrees Celsius. The *haus sik* was closed and it was dark now and still raining heavily. Aspirin, chloroquine and bathing—everybody took it in turns to look after him. Pella was still sulking, agreeing no doubt with the actions of the ancestors.

Plagues of flying termites have been providing a thick, dry sauce for our dinners, settling everywhere, flying towards the lit-up places, a seething mass of moving life. Jan and Mishka have been turned off their food. Nadya is doing her shift of nursing Numndi and I have been eating my dinner, rejecting awareness of the complete misery of the debacle. We have got beyond being upset by a mere plague of termites on a wet night in a shabby hut falling sideways into the mud, with Numndi at death's door in the next house. We just accept each new setback, numbly.

18 September

This Saturday started with a beautiful orange dawn creeping across the mountain tops. Rafal usually encourages us to admire the dawn, and this morning I blessed him for it. The leaves of the breadfruit trees are now clear and bright, shining in the early-morning sun. Rafal has gone to Numndi's house, rushing through the coffee garden at the sound of Pella's whistling call.

Numndi has recovered full consciousness and now lies groaning and gasping on a cold rock, saying that his *skinhot* has gone, but he has a huge belly-ache which ends at the neck. I removed him from the rock and wrapped him in a blanket, advising Pella to make him warm tea. *Tipokai* has let him off lightly, with just a stern warning, leaving Pella as the victor. I bet that was Olek, scoring another difficult victory over those other ancestors. He would have seen Pella's point of view, but Olek also knows just how much Numndi means to us.

Nadya goes about her daily duties with Pella and the women—washing in the river and going to the gardens with them. They are all planting new gardens now, after the long dry. Everywhere are circular patches of burnt and slashed forest, with new anti-pig fences, waiting to be planted by the women, gardens which will feed them for the next three years. I must go and take some photos. I'm going home soon now, leaving this place for good. I shall photograph Nadya and Pella working and planting, bums up, heads down, moving rapidly on the steep slope which makes me lose my balance even when standing on it.

20 September

Yesterday, Voy, Nadya and Jan went off to the Mabege country for an unspecified number of days. Mishka graciously consented to stay here and keep me company. They took with them only Kunjil, the boy from Tigi, and three big packs. The rain has gone and it is hot and sunny again.

Numndi has risen from his deathbed and comes to chat, telling me that actually he had not intended to keep the girl who had come and caused his illness. He had wanted to give her away, perhaps in *moka*.

Would she, I wondered, be presented on a stick like that white *kapul*?

He went on to assure me that Pella would not really be upset by another wife and she should have realised that, as number one wife, she would be able now to loaf around the house making *bilums* and send the new wife to work in the gardens. In the past he had had such a number two wife and when he had thrown her out because of her loose behaviour with other men, Pella had cried. Numndi, even in his severely weakened state, made everything sound so reasonable I found myself simply nodding in agreement with him.

This time Pella really had behaved so much against her own self-interest that her own mother had been angry with her, telling her not to be so stupid. So Numndi says.

1 October

We've given the children an extra three weeks' holiday, totally without misgivings, and I have decided to go back with them, or soon after them, so these are my last weeks here. It should put a different complexion on things, sharpen my feelings about the place. Jan and Mishka have gone to the bush with Agena and Anis, to find bark for *skin dewi* to wear in Australia. They have taken supplies—rice, dried milk and breadfruit, a little medicine and a blanket each— and they will come back in two or three days time.

Nadya is jealous and angry that she was not allowed to go because of Agena being there, but with difficulty I stood firm on that one. She has just mooched off to the gardens to work, gossip and giggle. And to complain about what a controlling tyrant I am.

Voy is feeling nauseous, and I sit in the hot, oppressive afternoon, looking out on the twin peaks opposite, shrouded heavily with smoke and general afternoon haze, and think that soon all this will be a sort of movie in my memory. The people's faces will blend more and more into their soft mountains as time mists over the sharper lines of reality.

We shall forget the constant pressure of jostling crowds; of jealous factions; of people wanting medicine, pointing to their stomachs, their mouths, their babies, pointing, motioning; of men beautifully dressed in their handsome *skin dewi* and *tanget* leaves but wanting shorts, shirts, smokes, shoes, watches and radios—all the trappings of our culture. But we will never forget Numndi and Pella or any of the family: Kints the grandfather; Dokta, frail and intellectual; Ruminj, forever trying to become a councillor and forever missing out; the sad-eyed Ping, dreaming her secret life.

On Friday all of us went to Hagen—Voy in a filthy mood, the children silent, me sulking as usual in response to his moroseness. But we reached Hagen after an interminable and pleasureless drive and then we all made up, as usual, and had lunch and took our filthy, exhausted selves off to Ulya, to see John and

Edith Watts again. Mrs Watts had been robbed that morning, half an hour before we arrived. She had been bringing the pay from the bank in town when her car was stolen from her by six men—a real hold-up. Why couldn't we have arrived at the same time, surprised the robbers and somehow saved Mrs Watts? Well, we didn't, and our friends were in deep shock.

They saw it as an omen. 'It is time for us to leave,' said John Watts. 'Our time here is finishing.'

We decided to cook the dinner, trying to help and be unobtrusive under the circumstances—not an easy task. The cook was at a loss to know why he wasn't doing the dinner. And then, after all that trouble, John Watts was not impressed with the cabbage rolls we had decided to cook as an exotic treat. He said he had never eaten such food and why should he start now, especially after they had been robbed? Edith told him not to be so rude in front of us when we were trying to please. We made a silent resolve not to try to cook again.

But the small ceremony of washing in a nice bathroom, perfuming and adorning ourselves for dinner at a table with conversation and candles had cheered us up and we eventually cheered up our hosts. Edith Watts ate a double portion of the cabbage rolls, declared them to be delicious and told John he was missing out because of his own narrow-mindedness. While remaining stubbornly opposed to the culinary innovation in his life, he was becoming mellow on whisky. So were we. The garden stretches, cool and quiet, full of cascading flowers and white doves. The house is old, with odd corridors and secret rooms, and nooks and crannies and double beds with laundered sheets. The coffee is in a silver pot and there is plenty of it. It is another world, a refuge, an oasis of charm and sanity. 'Ulya'—I'm sure it must mean haven with white doves.

11 October

So now we're back in Rulna and the countdown begins: three days to go, then two. And the children get nervous, trying to extract the last minutes of their beloved Rulna. Voy is becoming fractious, a radio and a tape-recorder have been stolen. He is always on the watch now, like a tiger—never relaxing. He has to go to the bush or up the mountains to relax and think, and this is what he does, taking Dokta with him, or Nadya or Jan. I went with him today to Palge. We lazed by the mountain river, the Mogilpin, and went over the theme of his work again. Why did these tribes take on Christianity, and how much did they actually take on, anyway? They often refer to their *tipokais* as 'Lord God', but the ancestors seem to perform the same function as they always did, Lord God notwithstanding.

Then we talked about home, our home: who would sleep where; how we could arrange everything; how we would feel back there, having to cope with life back in Canberra. We watched women bent under the weight of their loaded *bilums* cross the river on the high log bridge, silhouetted against the sky and the high trees, as we lay below on the stones, knowing that this sight was already etching into our memories because we were nearing the end.

22 October

The children have gone, amid a storm of suppressed emotion. They announced to people that they would not cry, and so all agreed that they too would not cry. Tears nevertheless appeared as the children, neatly dressed, once again crammed themselves and their possessions into the back of the jeep for the last bumpy climb up that mountain road: Jan in his long socks, Mishka still in his blue and yellow tracksuit, and Nadya in a dress, her safety pins faithfully dangling round her neck. That road must imprint itself into our memories for the rest of our lives: the steep drop on one side, the deep, smoky hollows and the changing colours of the receding mountains.

The timeless procession, walking up and down, moved to the edge of the precipice as we passed. They were staring, smiling: the women with crooked elbows clutching their long loads above their bent heads, their babies curled up and asleep in colourful *bilums*, the large child astride the mother's neck or emerging from a sling on her side; the husband, standing and clutching his bow and arrows, his axe stuck into his *skin dewi*, his two-cornered hat framing the handsome bearded face. Often they sit there, on the edge of the road, cooking some taro or sweet potato on small fires, or washing their babies in the mountain streams which ripple, clean and cold, over the road. Tall, wild sunflowers frame the view—a bright foreground against the gentle greys and blues of the mountain backdrop.

During this trip one week ago, the children had sat more silent than usual, not even fighting for space, thinking heavily that this was really their last time. For me, now, it is countdown. My feelings are mixed. I want to go home; all my voices tell me our time here is up. We must go back to our lives. These people must live their lives again, untroubled by jealous comparisons with the image of the white family living with the trappings of white culture and access to a seemingly wonderful and mysterious world, a world which, we know, will destroy as it touches. But as we approach that other world, our world, I know I will always be disturbed by periods of longing for this place and for the people whose lives we have been allowed to share so closely.

30 October

Voy is morose again, thinking of himself alone here when I am gone, a *redskin* without his *redskin meri*.

Numndi, Pella and Kints come constantly, eyes filled with tears, to make speeches. What will they do, they say, when they can't see Rafal running and playing and sharing their food? Is he not their baby boy? Does he not know their talk rather than ours? How will Pella work her garden or her *bilum* when all she can do is cry for Rafal? I promise, uselessly, to send photos, to write letters, to send presents; I give them our last grimy bedsheets and clothes; still they are not comforted. I say that tomorrow we will buy them four ducks to *mu-mu* for their health and ours.

Then Kints gets sick and Voytek carries the old man to the *haus sik* in the car to get his leg treated. Kints is so pleased with this treatment that he thinks he will remain in the car for the rest of the day, which he does.

A few people are sick now. Pit and her baby have a high fever; the baby has been ill for a week now. A few people have malaria, and the nurse says it is now another kind, a worse kind, not responsive to the drugs they have down there.

Numndi and Pella beg to have Rafal stay one or two nights and I agree, sorry that they are losing their precious white boy. I load them with the paraphernalia which I think is necessary for one tiny child to go and stay the night: bottles, nappies, a sheet, a mattress. How crazy! Their babies need nothing but a few leaves in the bottom of a colourful bush *bilum*, and a nice steady milk supply from the mother's breast, which never seems to run dry.

15 November—Cairns

Now, suddenly, that life has gone. Rulna is no more. A memory. Another life. Here we are in Cairns, interned in a caravan park, all fighting for space in one small van. The sea, it is true, swishes and roars on the other side of the casuarinas and coconut trees. The owls call at night and the crocodiles, say the other campers, bark. Rafal toddles around the environs, solemnly bemused and distracted by all the vehicle life here: motorbikes with jet engines which roar off into the dawn, old Holdens, new Datsuns, four-wheel drives with spare tyres on their roofs, one Jaguar. We have bought him a small red plastic motorbike to help him to forget Rulna. But first thing in the morning he goes out and calls for Pella, waiting for a few seconds for her secret whistling noise, coaxing him to come to her through the coffee gardens. His hard adjustment has begun.

We talk about Rulna, about my goodbye party, and Rafal. It rained, as usual, just as the ducks were raised from the ground. It rained on Ruminj's speeches; it rained on my tears and my spears—yes, I was presented with many, many spears decorated with red flowers, fur bands for my head and *kina* shells for my neck, with tufts of fur at the end. Rafal was too. Numndi and Pella and Moni gave me a huge *bilum* full of presents tightly wrapped in foolscap and bound with my plastic masking tape: *purr purr* (skimpy grass skirts), other *bilums*, necklaces, armlets, cloth made from beaten wood.

Kopi—the village simpleton whom I had always more or less ignored, taking his presence for granted but offering the standard rations simply because he was there—Kopi, too, brought gifts: all his carefully made body decorations.

I was touched. And caught out—what could I give them in return? I rushed inside, madly scrabbling through the last of my possessions and found a torch, hair-cutting scissors, a few towels, a fancy purse, two bottles of oil, gold bottles with embossed lids, a ripped mosquito net, two sarongs and my boots. These I distributed with due ceremony—'backing' their gifts.

And the next morning we left. Forever. Moka was crying and it touched me because he had never imposed on us for anything since the hookworm incident, and I had always liked him from a distance. Our own small family came with us to the airport at Hagen: Numndi, Pella, Moni and Numndi's two little girls, Greta and Sana. The last long, bumpy drive. I glanced up at the low cloud, imagining that I could see the ancestors lined up, gravely noting our departure from their domain. Could Olek follow us out of the valley, and continue to shepherd his children in the wider world? Or would he stay there with the Gamegai, hovering in the cosy white mists of Rulna?

We were all silent, suffering from the separation and the knowledge that the next meeting, if it ever happened, would be different, more distressing. Rafal would be big, shy, oblivious of the place and the people with whom he had spent the first two vital years, of the knees he had sat on, of Pella's husky voice which had lulled and soothed him, of her secret tracks through the coffee garden to Numndi's house, of the small children playing marbles in the dust with pebbles. The sounds of the *moka*, droning across the smoky hollows. The sounds of the forest birds, of the river. The sounds of Rulna.

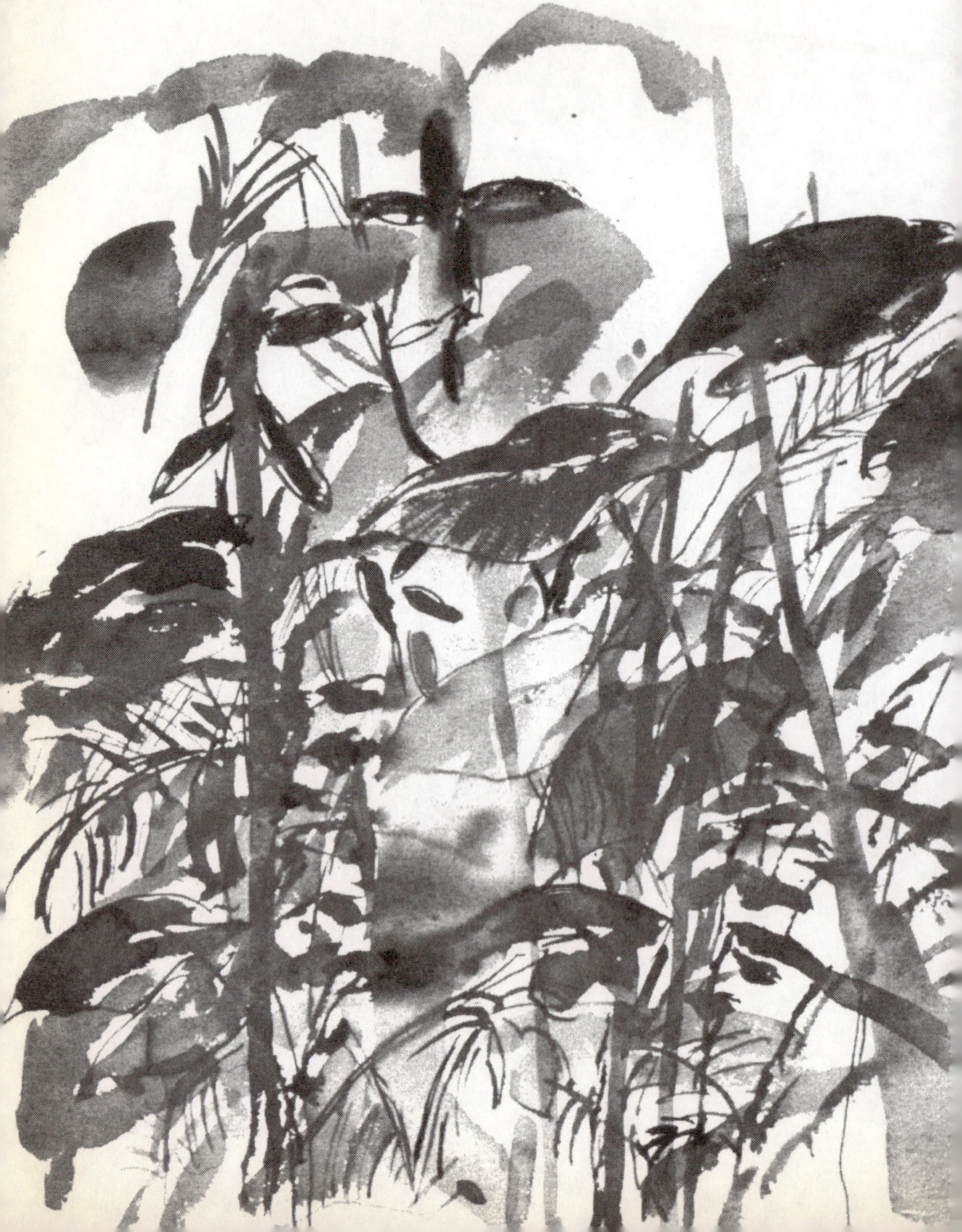

Another Life

Soon after we left, Numndi joined us in Cairns. He was unnerved by the flight and very glad to be on the ground. Rafal ran towards him and Numndi wept noisily as he swept him up and stroked the curly head into his neck. We all wept, relieved, as the anxiety and Rulna-sickness came flooding out. We made a sobbing spectacle of ourselves in the small airport in Cairns. Numndi's arrival was miraculous confirmation to us that the whole of our life in Rulna had not been a dream that was just making us sick with longing. Numndi had been the centre of our lives there and now he had come to live in the caravan with us. Rafal stopped his whingeing and became calm again.

We put our energy into making sure that Numndi saw everything, to have stories to tell the others around his hearth, to make his trip worthwhile. We took him to the crocodile park and he was impressed with the great beasts, with their snapping jaws. Despite the presence of crocodiles in the Sepik River, the people of Rulna had never seen one.

Numndi had always heard about the sea. And here we were on the Great Barrier Reef. We spent the day on a boat and he scrutinised the brilliant striped fish as they flashed noiselessly around the coral gardens. Perhaps he was comparing their colours to the vivid birds of paradise. He may have wanted to catch some. He made no comment. Perhaps he was thinking of how they would taste in a *mu-mu*. I sat back and lazily gazed at the misty islands, the sun stirring my fantasies. I was thinking of Voy, still in Rulna, and I was enjoying the little daydream, missing his sweetness, forgetting his moodiness. The boat was rocking enticingly, encouraging my dream. I wanted to be with him.

Two weeks after Christmas we went south again, to our house in Canberra, to wait for Voy. Once again I waited and he didn't come. There was no magic paper-burning ceremony to tell me when he was not arriving. I waited at the airport, dressed up as I hadn't dressed for years, watching the arrivals gate. I drove home alone, my glamour unnoticed, and uninformed about why he had not arrived. I was struggling to suppress tears which were blurring my driving vision.

He came at night, two days later, and woke me. Once again we were all together. Numndi was sleeping with Mishka and Rafal, not to be lonely. Every morning he got up at dawn and made a fire. He started to fret, away from Pella, away from the politics and the pigs, the gossip and constant activity of the clan members, away from Rulna. Our food was too varied for him, and he said our sweet potatoes were too slushy. '*Nogat strong*,' he said, stubbornly refusing to eat them. He missed the stringy, dry Rulna type of *kau kau*. He stopped eating properly.

Then we heard that Kints was ill. Numndi went back. Kints died, leaving unheard-of instructions that nobody was to wail or tear their hair for him. He just wanted a celebration. A big party. His wish was honoured, but the Gamegai were left without a leader. Kints had been a major visionary, a figure who even in his weak old age had been able to exert authority, to see his tribe in larger terms. He had negotiated pacts with the first missionary, with rival clans, with enemy tribes, and finally, with his own ancestors. Voy has written all about Kints in *Line to Heaven*.

And then Moka, the quiet man who had hookworm, died and the Gamegai blackened their faces, got out their shields and cassowary plumes and went to war. They blamed the death on the Menimbi tribe. They said the Menimbis had poisoned him.

•

Jan was the first one of us to go back three years later. It was he who had brought back the news of Moka's death. And then Nadya and Jan went back together, the next Christmas holidays, acting as guides for a Polish actor, Mariusz, who wanted to see New Guinea. Nadya wrote:

Coming back to Rulna was different for me, painfully different. When I was there before, the people were mine and I was theirs. I had never wanted to leave. I had only wanted to be a Rulna girl, stay and marry my boyfriend Agena, and dig sweet potatoes. My family with all their possessions, their sophistication, had been an embarrassment to me. I had tried to deny my background. Rulna was the most important part of my life, even long after I left. All I wanted to do was go back there.

Eventually it changed. My life altered its course. I threw in my dreams about the village as I threw in my childhood.

I couldn't stop crying at the faces of Numndi and Pella, running up the road towards me and Jan. But my immediate impression was that this was an isolated place, a small valley, in the middle of high, dark mountains. I was conscious of the actor, Mariusz; of having to translate for him, to explain to him. It made me more of an outsider, like a guide.

The small valley, we read in her letter, was suffering, in the throes of war. Meta, the giggling teenager, had been killed. Moni had gone back to Tigi. Agena had been presented to her but he had lost his old magic. Everyone was nervous. There was no *moka*, no *tanim het*. Numndi was protecting them, monitoring all their movements. Although no battle action was visible, there was agitation in the air and on everyone's faces.

> Our conversations with Numndi, Pella and Dokta drift from small talk to what has been happening in Rulna over the last few months. Tribal war. It has been completely dominating their lives. All of them are touched by it, under the threat of it: wives, children, pigs, gardens.

Nadya was weighed down by the changes she saw. She got malaria and Jan nursed her, knowing what to do, remembering the dosages.

•

The war finished and some Gamegai moved to Tigi to protect their conquered lands. The young and confident Councillor Kongga died and, aware of the approach of death, instructed the other Gamegai that nobody should go to war over it. His wish prevailed, and so did peace. Pri is now the Councillor, replacing Kongga, but they have never found another Kints as leader. Such men are rare.

As for us, the children are no longer children, except for Rafal. Nadya became a singer. In 1994, with a PNG record company, she put out an album of songs she and Mishka had written, based on their life in Rulna—songs they had put together over the years, collected from refrains and rhythms and themes of Rulna. They were taken on a highly publicised tour round PNG, including Mount Hagen.

Numndi and Pella heard of them on the mountain *bik-mousing* grapevine. They set off on the long walk, up the mountain range and down into the Hagen Valley. They arrived, after three days, at the luxury hotel in Hagen where the stars were being accommodated. Mishka, worrying about how he and Nadya could contact them, suddenly spotted them out the window and rushed downstairs, the years of bottled-up dreams and anxiety about finding each other boiling over.

Here was their very own Nadya, a celebrity, in a hotel in Mount Hagen. And Dokta Miki. Nadya had become a grass roots star in the highlands, singing in pidgin, amazing and amusing the crowd with her rapid highland vernacular learned as a child in Rulna. The concerts were crowded. Barriers were put up to control the crowds. But Numndi and Pella were the real stars, the couple from the bush who had taught this passionate young performer her first verses in their language. They had their own table, next to the stage, and were introduced by Dokta Miki, the compere. Once again, Nadya was theirs and they were hers.

They moved into the hotel room, despite the furious protests of the manager at having to accommodate non-paying, shoe-less guests from the deep bush. They stayed for the week, attending all the concerts as the special introduced guests, the originators and inspiration for the songs.

Pella had her first hot bath. '*Kai-yaye!*' she shouted,

refusing to take off her lap-lap and not allowing the hot water past her knees. Two more Gamegai arrived; the men slept in Dokta Miki's room with him and the women with Nadya. To eat, they all went to Raima's and made a *mu-mu* in the ground outside his house. And as more and more Gamegai arrived, the *mu-mus* became the gathering place.

Mishka's video footage of the Hagen experience, plus a few reverse-charge phone calls from the hotel, convinced us to take the big step. We decided to throw caution to the winds, brave the new dangers of the highland roads, and take Rafal back to Rulna. We started to plan.

Nadya's concert tours, and the publicity attached to them, set the ball rolling. Six months after the phone calls from the hotel, we returned.

Nadya was still in Moresby completing her recording. Mishka had returned to Australia to bring his girlfriend Plaxy to meet Numndi and Pella. We all arrived in Hagen and tried to devise a way of getting to Rulna, minimising the much-discussed risks of the highways. Notorious robber gangs (*raskols*) were staging hold-ups along the roads, virtually unchecked by the impoverished provincial police force. Killing for cargo, stealing the trucks and raping the women passengers was becoming commonplace.

Our first step was to find Raima, which was easy. He was still living in his hut on the side of the runway, even wearing the same t-shirt. Raima volunteered not only to find us a vehicle but also to drive us there. After days of fruitless rendezvous with vehicle owners we braved the road in an old, brakeless ute which we had hired more out of desperation than discernment. We tried to leave early, before the robbers would be awake. That was my idea, thinking no doubt of home, where robbers all sleep in. But Raima was impressed with the suggestion. We took as many locals as we could cram into the back, including the convicted *raskol* Ten (Raima's son) to protect us. And off we went, back along the road to Rulna. But Raima did not go to Rulna. He turned off before the Rulna road, because somehow he knew that Numndi and Pella would be in Tigi.

It was a long drive. Raima drove fast, slowing down for no-one, until he reached territory where the truck could only move at bumping speed. But already here the sense of danger had abated. Here he was known. At this point the anticipation in all of us was making us completely silent with tension. Little groups kept appearing from behind the trees and staring. And then an excited gathering came running up a shallow riverbed. Numndi and Pella emerged from the shouting crowd. Suddenly Rafal was whisked from the back of the truck and carried away on their shoulders. I saw his surprised face looking back at me as they shouted and cried with joy at finding their lost baby.

Then it was our turn. We were clambering down, being half-pulled. They found my patch of grey hair. They laughed at Voytek's extra poundage, at Dokta Miki's new beard. They swarmed all over Nadya. Plaxy was trying to take photos and Dokta Miki was struggling to stay upright to video the welcome.

'Where's Jan?'

'He has a *meri* and a *piccaninny* on the way. He couldn't come.'

'Oh, *sori*!'

I showed them the photos of Jan and Bem, and their Indian wedding, with Jan riding on the white horse and Bem, covered in her family's silk and gold, looking like a princess. They looked as good as any *moka*.

Numndi and Pella looked the same. Pella even had a baby at her breast. The baby was called Miki. We were taken to Mikel Kewa's house to sleep. Tigi looked so beautiful. The evening mists surrounded us, shot through with the late afternoon sun. We could hear the roar of the *moka* through the forest and gradually, in small groups, painted warriors and women came along the track. Some knew us, though we couldn't recognise them behind the paint as they rushed at us, laughing and gesticulating. Pri, Ruminj, Pugga, Anis, Moni, Kewa, Maga, Meri Ko—our old friends. It was the end of a great journey.

But there was someone missing. Dokta. He was dead. For most of us it was Numndi and Pella we had really missed. But it was Dokta whom Voy had been waiting to see. Dokta had been his friend, adviser, confidant. They had always been together. The thought of him not being there had not occurred to Voy, who had been corresponding with Dokta until fairly recently. Then the letters had stopped. And it must have been round about that time that the *tipokais* had taken Dokta away from his wife and his little house by the high stream. They had always tried to get him, those *tipokais*. They had stalked him until they got him.

Some of the Gamegai still lived down at Rulna, but many, including Numndi and Pella and their two daughters, had migrated to Tigi to be less remote. The road to Rulna had become permanently blocked and was undriveable. To go to Rulna now, one had to undertake the three-day walk or else walk from Tigi, several strenuous hours under a hot sun. The mission had closed down soon after we left, as the isolation had taken its toll on Father Josef.

Now the changing weather patterns, the shocking drought and the frost killing the sweet potato crops over the last year, has started to attract some people back again, down to Rulna, where the frost doesn't come, where the river never ceases to flow, and where the pigs roam free. But there is no hope of relief supplies from town getting to Rulna, and one runaway fire in the slash and burning season set the forest ablaze.

The swidden gardens of Rulna, sheltered in the deep forests, can still yield crops, whereas the specially cultivated plots around Tigi are easier victims of rainless seasons and black frosts. The danger of forest fire when there is drought has prevented the people from attempting to slash and burn until the rain sets in again. Meanwhile, Peter Kewa has become the *dokta boy* at Rulna. Unthinkably, he has married a Jimmi woman and has three children. Mikel Kewa and his two wives have migrated and he is now the *dokta boy* in Tigi.

The next day Rafal was taken by Numndi and Pella to join the *moka*. Lovingly and proudly they painted him, stripping him of his trousers, despite his loud protests, and replacing them with the *tanget* leaves, the bark belt, a huge headdress, arm bracelets, necklets. And then he was in the line of men, between Pri and Mikel Kewa, his slim, pale thirteen-year-old arms linked with their dark sinewy men's forearms. Voy and I watched, standing beside Numndi and Pella, observing their prized boy doing the dance of the *moka*.

We had returned.

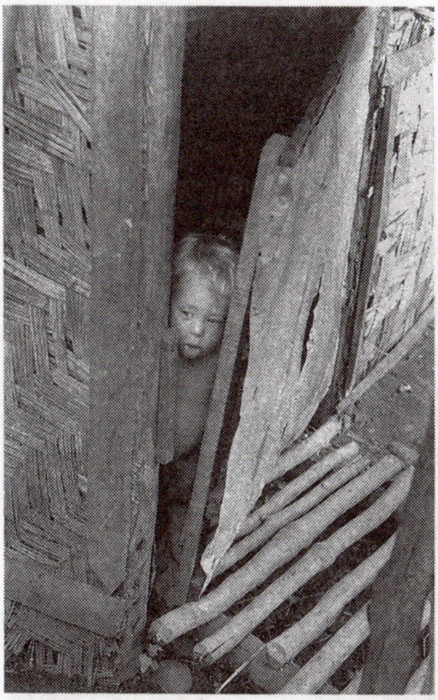

People and Places

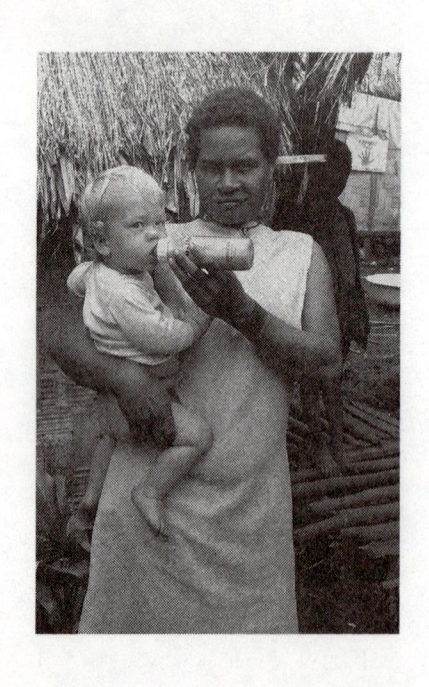

Agena   friend of Mishka whom Nadya thinks she would like to marry

Anis   Gamegai man caught seducing a married Palge woman

Bak   son of Ruminj

Boy (aka 'Wing Bean')   a guide

Brother Paul   Dutch Catholic missionary in Rulna

Dokta   one of Kints' sons and friend of Voy

Father Josef   Polish Catholic missionary in Rulna

Gabriel Kei   Rulna storekeeper

Greta   daughter of Pella and Numndi

Gris   son of Mabege bigman; friend of Nadya

Jimmi people   inhabitants of Jimmi Valley; short in stature, and subject to virulent malaria and skin diseases; most die young; build houses on stilts, surrounded by huge gardens

Jimmi Valley   two days walk from Rulna, across the Jimmi River

Kabuga   family cat

Kaip   Rulna church leader

Kant   village in the Jimmi area

Kawelka tribe   inhabitants of Tigi (see map p. 264); friendly with the Gamegai

Kints   grand old bigman of Rulna; father of Numndi, Ruminj, Dokta, Moka, Pugga, Kar, Raima and possibly others

Kongga   Dokta's new wife

Kongga, Councillor   Tigi official; rival of ex-Councillor Kuk

Kuk, Ex-Councillor   Tigi official; rival of Councillor Kongga
Kumu Toga   Minister for Lands
Kunjil   boy from Tigi
Mak   father of Kunjil
Malu Malu   Mishka's pet *kapul*
Maria   lover of Rot
Meri Meta   friend of Nadya
Mikel Kewa   barefoot doctor
Moglam   seat of the area High Court
Moka   one of Kints' sons
Moni   Numndi's wife, Pella's younger sister and Nadya's friend
Mount Hagen   only local town with shops, post office, hospital, market and hostel; approximately four hours drive through the mountains
Numndi   befriends author's family and 'manages' them; husband of Pella, father of Sana and Greta
Palge tribe   inhabitants of forested Palge Mountains on other side of valley from Rulna (see map p. 264)
Panna   Rulna policeman
Pella   girl from Tigi who becomes sick in Rulna
Pella   Numndi's wife; assists with caring for Rafal
Peter Kewa   Ruminj's adult stepson and a local *dokta boy*
Pig   Councillor Kongga's brother
Ping   wife of Ruminj
Pri   Village Court Magistrate
Punk   Kawelka boy adopted by Gamegai as a baby
Purewei, Councillor   son of Wei

Puruwei Kuri   Rulna politician

Raima   one of Kints' sons, living in Mount Hagen

Rokembo   family name of Kints and his relatives

Rot   Jan's friend and lover of Maria

Ruminj   Kints' son and husband of Ping

Sana   daughter of Pella and Numndi

Tigi   nearby mountain village, only accessible on foot

Tigi tribe   another set of mountain dwellers (see map p. 264)

Tipeka tribe   another set of mountain dwellers (see map p. 264)

Tsandiap   beautiful high place across the Jimmi River

Wahg   village man, friend of Kints

Wamp   assistant to Mikel Kewa

Wei   grand old bigman of Palge

Winimp   family dog

Distribution of Tribes

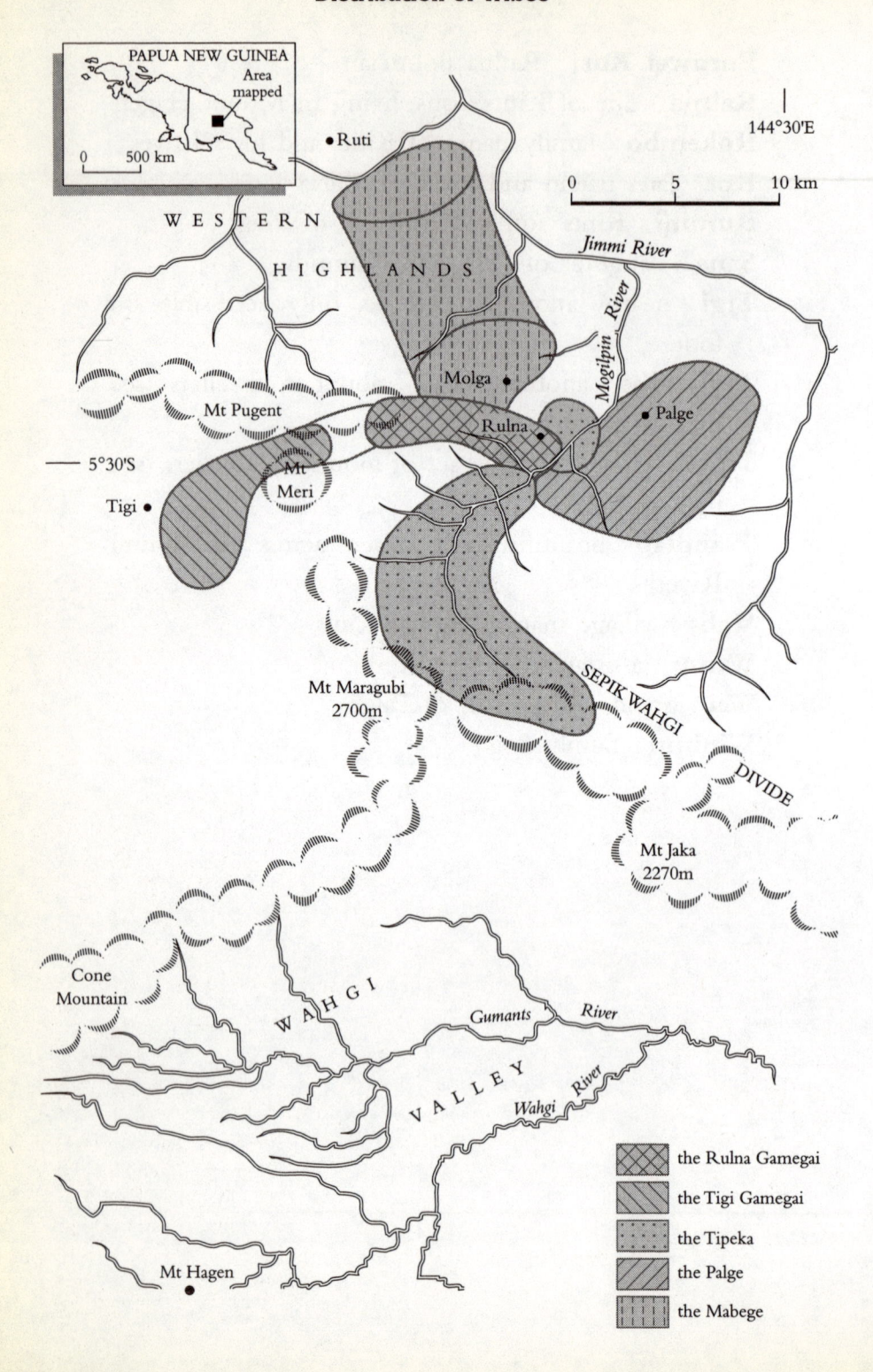

PAPUA NEW GUINEA
Area mapped
0 500 km

144°30'E
0   5   10 km

Ruti

WESTERN HIGHLANDS

Jimmi River

Mogilpin River

Molga

Mt Pugent

Rulna

Palge

5°30'S

Mt Meri

Tigi

Mt Maragubi
2700m

SEPIK WAHGI DIVIDE

Mt Jaka
2270m

Cone Mountain

WAHGI

Gumants River

VALLEY

Wahgi River

Mt Hagen

- the Rulna Gamegai
- the Tigi Gamegai
- the Tipeka
- the Palge
- the Mabege

Rulna Village and Surrounds

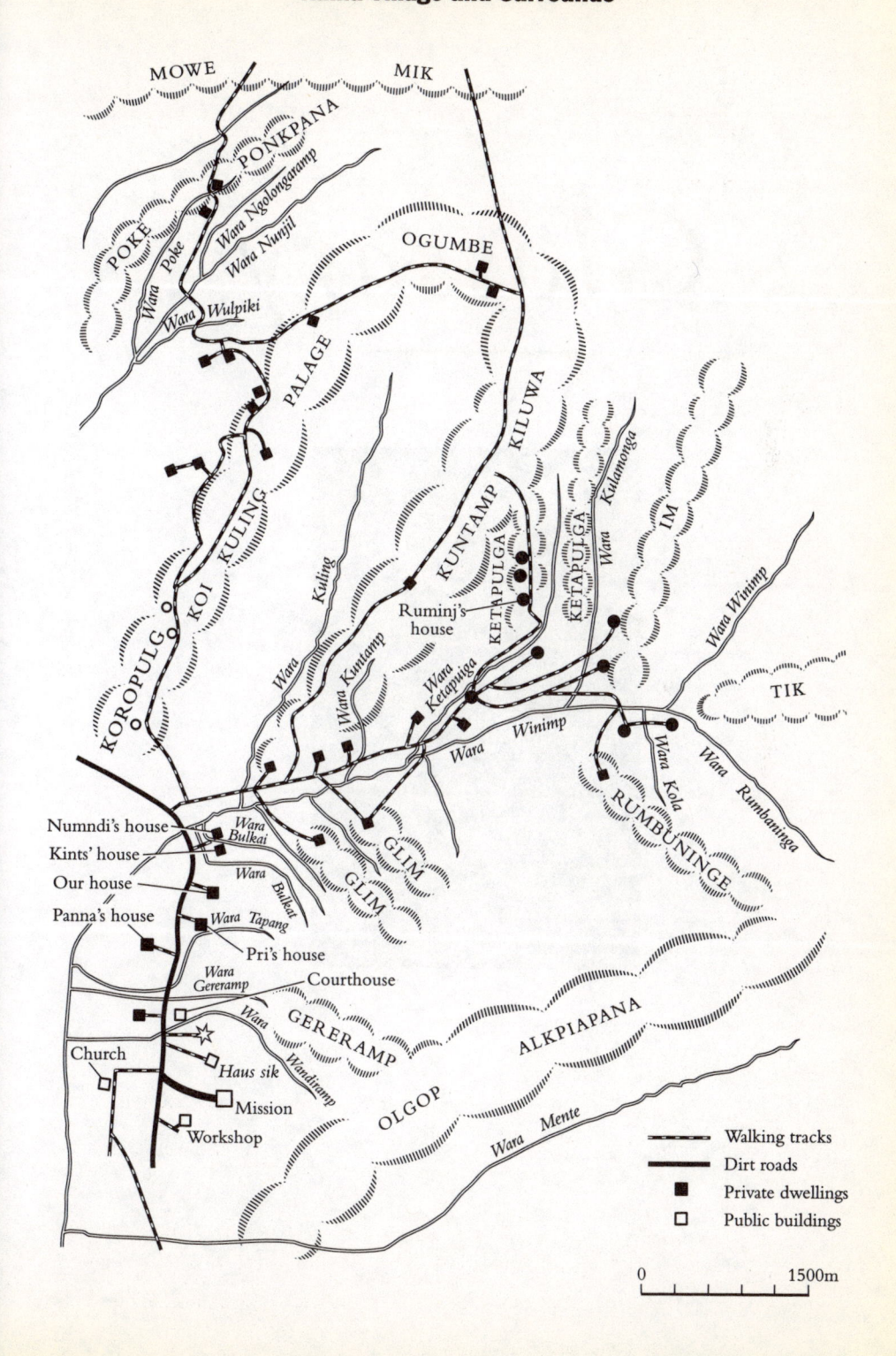

Glossary

ambkundr woman with red skin

bal front panel of *skin dewi*

bik-mousing calling out of names to receive portions of pig; also, form of long-distance communication which involves calling from hill to hill

bilum large net bag, most commonly used for carrying a baby, but also for supplies and personal possessions

Gamegai name of local tribe in Rulna

greasing seducing

gris fat

guria earthquake

gutpela taim good time

haus sik Rulna nurses' station

het i pen na skin ut tu headache and temperature

k-lapping a form of dancing, considered sexy

kabuga okay

kapiac breadfruit

kapul black and white striped possum-like creature, with a long tail much coveted as a neck decoration

kau kau sweet potato

kiap Australian patrol officer

kina local currency

kints grasshopper

kit bad, no good, danger

kunai a type of grass used for thatching

kundu long, waisted, wooden drum

kus kus fur possum fur

lapoon old woman

lapoon finis woman past child-bearing
malu malu mud; also a term of endearment meaning 'soft'
mamiok tapioca
marita mu-mu pandanus fruit feast
marita vermillion fruit of the pandanus
MelpaRulna dialect
meri bilong wok a hard-working woman
moka ritual of one tribe giving pigs to another
mu-mu feast of feasts with elaborate rituals attached; also a form of cooking
numndi lone survivor of tribal war
nuntz nettle leaf with healing properties
olga surprise bonus
outim throwing out, getting rid of
pamuk meri whore
pek pek wara diarrhoea
pidgin bastardised form of English, used throughout PNG and the Pacific for communication between English-speakers and the local people
pig-bel endemic and often fatal food poisoning from pig meat
pit pit a long, soft cane grass which, when beaten out and woven into panels, is nailed into place to form the walls of huts
plani sik piccaninny plenty of sick children
plour damper pancakes
pri vomit
redskins 'white' people; could be mistaken for ancestors

rop kunda   thick bush cane
ruminj   centre pole of shelter
sangumas   evil spirits
sik mun   menstruation
sing sing   celebration
skin dewi   wide belt worn by village men
tanget   bum
tanim het   courting ritual
tipokai   vigilant ancestor
tipokit   angry ghost, bush spirit
tok wara   talk without substance
toya   small unit of local currency
wantok   extended family, clan member, relative

Acknowledgements

I have had a lot of help with turning what was a handwritten diary and a few letters into a book, and I want to thank those who have encouraged and assisted me with inspired suggestions: Margot Sutton, Anna and Vida Carden-Coyne, Virginia Wilton, Jill Kitson, Suzie Eisenhuth, Plaxy McCulloch, Hannah Kay, Aviva Ziegler, Robin Anderson, Amanda Ducker, the late Nick Brash of Bow Press and Matthew Richardson from Halstead Press. Also Sandra Gross and my friends from the desert painting group who listened to me read around the camp fire at night; Caroline Lurie and Pauline McGuire of Hodder Headline for their very expert assistance in editing; and my agent, Gaby Naher of Hickson Associates, for being so enthusiastic.

And of course I want to thank my own beloved family, who have been good-natured enough to allow me to tell our story with full frankness, and particularly Voytek, who made the whole thing happen.